THE WORLD ALMANAC BOOK OF WHY

EXPLANATIONS FOR ABSOLUTELY EVERYTHING

World Almanac for Kids™

WORLD ALMANAC BOOKS

World Almanac books may be purchased in bulk at special discounts for sales promotion, corporate gifts, fund-raising, or educational purposes. Special editions can also be created to specifications. For details, contact the Special Sales Department, 307 West 36th Street, 11th Floor, New York, NY 10018 or info@skyhorsepublishing.com.

Published by World Almanac, an imprint of Skyhorse Publishing, Inc., 307 West 36th Street, 11th Floor, New York, NY 10018.

www.skyhorsepublishing.com

10 9 8 7 6 5 4 3 2 1

Cover design by David Ter-Avanesyan
Cover photographs by Shutterstock and NASA
Text by Emily Dolbear

Library of Congress Cataloging-in-Publication Data is available on file.

Print ISBN: 978-1-5107-6858-1
Ebook ISBN: 978-1-5107-6859-8

Printed in China

CONTENTS

ANIMALS

The animal kingdom is as big and diverse as our world. Furry, slippery, feathered, winged, horned, scaly, glowing animals come in all sizes. They can be plentiful or rare. They can be our best friends. They can help and guide us. They can help feed us. In the wild, they also amaze, mystify, and terrify us. Why are we so scared of sharks? Why are ladybugs red? Why do cats knead? No time to "paws"—read on for answers!

BIG-EARED AND BUSHY-TAILED

What makes a CHEETAH so fast?

Cheetahs are the racing car of the wild. They can sprint more than 70 miles (113 km) an hour. It takes them just three seconds to reach that speed. Long powerful legs, a flexible spine, and a long tail make them quick and steady. Their claws provide a lot of traction. They are the world's fastest land animals.

Why do PANDA BEARS poop so much?

If you can believe it, this forest dweller poops 50 times a day. What goes in must come out. Panda bears eat about 30 pounds (14 kg) of bamboo shoots and leaves daily. They are able to digest only about one-fifth of that. That's why they feed as many as 16 hours a day. More than one million years ago, the panda bear used to eat meat as well as plants. Scientists are not sure why its digestive system never adapted.

Why does a female KANGAROO have a pouch?

A baby kangaroo, or joey, can't see or hear at birth. It's the size of a mere jellybean. The mother nurses and protects her baby in the pouch, where it even pees and poops. The joey pokes its head out at about four months to nibble grass. At six months, the joey hops around for food before returning. A few months after that, it's time for the young kangaroo to fly the coop, or hop the pouch, for good.

What is the difference between BISON and BUFFALO?

Millions of wild bison used to roam the American West. Buffalo are found in South Asia and Africa. They are two very different animals. The American bison has a hump at the shoulders and short horns. The buffalo has no hump and large horns. Songs and history often call American bison buffalo. Just to make things more confusing, there is also a European bison.

THE WHYS OF SOME STANDOUT ANIMAL TRAITS

All living things have special physical characteristics that have adapted over time to help them survive in the wild. Some land animals have physical features that are out of the ordinary.

Elephant
What? Big ears
Why? Blood circulates through the large surface area of the floppy ears, helping heat to escape and keeping the animal cool.

Giraffe
What? Purple tongue
Why? The tongue's dark color comes from a pigment called melanin that reduces the risk of sunburn on this delicate part of the body.

Lion
What? Mane
Why? The mane of an adult male attracts potential mates by announcing good genes that will provide strong and healthy cubs.

Polar Bear
What? Whitish fur
Why? Transparent hairs reflect visible light and make the bear more able to blend in to its snow-covered surroundings, allowing it to stalk and feed on seals.

Porcupine
What? Quills
Why? Long sharp quills on the back—as many as 30,000—help protect the rodent from predators.

ON THE FLY

Why do BIRDS CHIRP so early in the morning?

Waking up at 4 a.m. is a challenge for most people. But not, apparently, for birds. Some call it the "dawn chorus." That's the sound of birds chirping their hearts out before the sun rises. It's mostly males, protecting their territories and attempting to attract a mate. It takes energy to sing so loudly. Strong trills and crescendos show strength to the competition.

Why does a FLAMINGO sleep standing on one leg?

The best answer seems to be because it takes less energy. Standing on one leg instead of two uses the muscles less. It also allows the flamingo to hold a steadier position while sleeping. Though it doesn't sound very comfortable, sleeping upright certainly works for this distinctive wading bird.

Why do some birds MIGRATE?

When the seasons change, so does the supply of food. Animals often travel a distance to where the food is. The longest bird migration is that of the Arctic tern. This slender, fish-eating bird migrates from pole to pole so it enjoys two summers each year. They breed in the Arctic during the summer and then fly to Antarctica. The round trip covers more than 20,000 miles (32,000 km).

Learn More

Go to National Audubon Society to find bird-watching tips and games.

- www.audubon.org/news/easy-ways-get-kids-birding

Why do certain BUTTERFLIES migrate?

Certain butterfly species migrate, just like some bird species. In North America, monarch butterflies go south for the winter to breed and north in the spring. Eastern populations winter in Texas, Florida, and Mexico. Western populations winter along the coast of California. Monarch butterflies migrating from Canada to Mexico and back again travel more than 6,000 miles (10,000 km).

Why are MOTHS most active at night?

Butterflies and moths have much in common. They are both flower pollinators. However, while butterflies feed during the day, most moths take the night shift. It's easier to find food while other creatures are asleep.

Why are LADYBUGS red?

The ladybug's main predators are birds. Its bright colors warn animals that it is poisonous. Being flashy to protect yourself might seem illogical. But these beetles thrive around the world so they must be doing something right. When attacked, the ladybug releases a substance that smells and tastes foul. That helps get the message across to stay away.

Does a FLYING SQUIRREL really fly?

A furry membrane called the patagium allows a flying squirrel to glide through the air. The small animal steers by moving its wrist bones, and it brakes with its long, flat tail. While these rodents are able to soar hundreds of feet from tall trees, they aren't real flyers. "Sailplaning squirrel" might be a more accurate name.

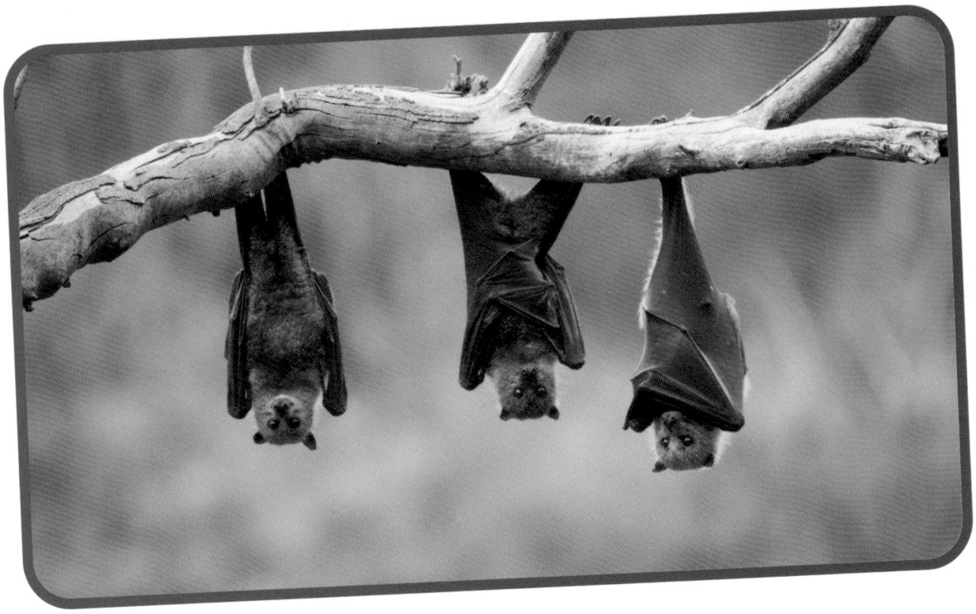

Why do BATS hang UPSIDE DOWN?

A bat's hind legs are not usually strong enough to support their body weight. As a bonus, taking off from the hanging position is easier for bats. Hanging by its feet allows a bat to rest effortlessly in a cave or hollow tree, making it safer from predators.

SEA THESE CREATURES

Why are DOLPHINS often considered the SMARTEST animals?

Compared to their body size, dolphins have very large brains. The only brain-to-body weight ratio higher is that of humans. But that's not all. These highly social animals communicate through a range of sounds. They use tools to solve problems. They can even recognize themselves in a mirror. Baby dolphins showed signs of this (like twirling or blowing bubbles) in front of a mirror earlier than children in a recent scientific study.

How do OYSTERS make PEARLS?

A natural pearl often starts out as a nasty parasite. Not a beautiful beginning. The parasite bores into the shell of the oyster. A mollusk naturally protects itself from the intruder by covering it with a secretion called nacre. An oyster produces about three layers of the rich, shimmering nacre daily. This eventually creates a natural pearl. It can take years to produce a pearl measuring only 1/5 inch (5 mm), which is why they are so rare. No two natural pearls are alike. Now, that's a thing of beauty.

Why are WHALES not considered fish?

Whales share the characteristics of other mammals. Like humans and other land mammals, whales breathe air with lungs (using their blowholes, instead of nostrils). They are warm-blooded. That means they keep a high body temperature even in the cold water. Whales have hair (though it's sparse). They give birth to live baby whales. And they produce milk to nurse their young. On the other hand, fish get oxygen through their gills. They are cold-blooded, which means their body temperature changes depending on their environment. Fish have scales and lay eggs.

Why do DEEP-SEA creatures GLOW in the dark?

About three-quarters of all deep-sea animals are bioluminescent. That means they are able to produce their own light. Glowing in the dark helps animals attract mates, catch prey, or stun predators in the open ocean.

Why do JELLYFISH sting?

These spineless sea creatures sting with their tentacles. Stinging helps the jellyfish catch its prey and defend itself. Jellyfish are found in all oceans. There are more than 200 species of jellyfish. Most live for only a few weeks or months. The poison released by their tentacles can stun small prey and hurt swimmers. But beware. The sting from a sea wasp jellyfish—found in waters near Australia, Philippines, and Vietnam—can kill a human in only a few minutes in very extreme cases.

Are CORALS animals?

Corals are small living creatures that attach to the ocean floor. People sometimes think they're plants, but they aren't. Unlike plants, corals don't make their own food. They often build up as coral reefs. The world's biggest and perhaps most beautiful coral reef is the Great Barrier Reef in Australia. It stretches more than 1,400 miles (2,300 km) off the northeast coast.

Changes in temperature, light, or nutrients can cause corals to eject the algae living on them. When this happens, the corals turn white. This is called coral bleaching. Mass coral bleaching events on the Great Barrier Reef have led to widespread coral loss. Rising sea temperatures caused by climate change is the leading cause.

Learn More

Go to Oceana to explore an encyclopedia of marine life.

- oceana.org/marine-life

(UN)COOL ANIMALS

Why do some DESERT ANIMALS bury themselves in the sand?

Many desert animals spend the day deep underground in burrows. No surprise there. It's just cooler and more humid. The animals come out at night after the sun goes down to hunt or forage for food.

How long can DESERT TORTOISES survive without water?

These reptiles can last up to a year without fresh water. That's one strong bladder.

Why don't KANGAROO RATS drink water?

Kangaroo rats eat mostly seeds, some stems or fruit, and the occasional insect. Their bodies convert seeds into the water they need to survive. For every seed consumed, they produce water half that weight. They never need to sweat or pant like other animals to cool down.

How do DESERT ANIMALS keep SAND out of their eyes?

Many desert dwellers have a nictitating membrane in their eyes. This transparent third eyelid protects their eyes from sand blowing in the desert. Nictitating membranes benefit many other animals, including sharks. To catch flying grains of sand, camels also have extra-long eyelashes.

How long can CAMELS survive without water?

Camels can go a week or sometimes longer without water. The secret to these desert animals is the hump. Depending on the species, camels have one or two. The humps don't store water, however. They store fat to nourish the camel. When they shrivel and sag, it is a sign that the camel hasn't eaten or drunk in a long time. A camel can lose a third of its body weight in water without becoming dehydrated. Camels can carry people and loads up to 1,000 pounds (450 kg).

THE WHYS OF SOME DESERT ANIMAL TRAITS

Adaptations over time help animals in the desert survive lack of water and extreme temperatures. Some of them have unusual physical features.

Fennec Fox

What? Tall ears

Why? Ears as large as one-fourth of the fox's length help disperse body heat.

Jerboa

What? Tall legs and short forearms

Why? Elongated hind legs allow the rodent to move quickly and conserve its energy in the heat.

Arabian Oryx

What? White fur and dark legs

Why? The coat of the white antelope reflects the desert sun when it is hot, and its legs darken to absorb more heat in the winter.

Australian Thorny Devil

What? Thorny spines

Why? Thorny spines channel the tiniest drops of water to the mouth of this small lizard in the desert.

Meerkat

What? Black eye patches

Why? Dark coloring around the eyes reduces glare of the sun so the African mongoose can better spot predators.

DANGER AHEAD

Why are some animals ENDANGERED?

Pollution, overfishing, and building are often responsible for an animal becoming endangered. Humans can harm the air, water, and habitat that a species needs to survive. For example, sea turtles are losing their beach nesting sites to humans using the beaches, and thousands are killed every year when they get caught in fishing nets. Individuals, organizations, and governments can work to prevent an animal from becoming extinct.

Learn More

Go to National Wildlife Federation to see a directory of endangered species.

- www.nwf.org

What is the difference between ENDANGERED and EXTINCT?

An animal is endangered when so few exist, the species is at risk of dying out completely. The species becomes extinct when this happens.

Why do people POACH endangered animals? (What is POACHING?)

Poaching has nothing to do with eggs for breakfast. Poaching is hunting or fishing an animal illegally. Endangered animals often provide food, fur, or ivory. That makes it valuable to poach animals, even if it endangers them.

Why do people poach SEA TURTLES?

Poachers hunt sea turtles for their meat, skin, and colorful shells. Some people eat sea turtle eggs—even though that's against the law in most countries. Let's agree it's best to stick with chicken eggs for omelets.

Why is the JAVAN RHINOCEROS critically endangered?

In the past, people hunted this huge animal for its horn, which is about 10 inches (25 cm) long. Hunting them has been illegal for a long time now, but there are only about 60 Javan rhinos left in the world today. They live in a protected national park in Java, Indonesia. This rare rhinoceros weighs as much as 5,000 pounds (2,200 kg). That's as heavy as a full-size pickup truck.

Why is the BALD EAGLE no longer an endangered species?

America's national bird is soaring once again. It's a lofty story. Bald eagles used to suffer from hunting and pesticides in most states. (Hawaii never had bald eagles. They've always been plentiful in Alaska.) After passage of the Endangered Species Act (ESA) in 1973, the national symbol joined the official list of endangered species. ESA programs bred bald eagles, protected their nesting sites, and prevented hunting. By 1995, bald eagles were no longer endangered. But the Bald Eagle Protection Act of 1940 continues to ban hunting, selling, or harming the majestic bird.

Q&A: A Remarkable Person

Jane Goodall

Scientist in Animal Behavior

When and where was she born? 1934, in London, England

Why did she hide for hours in her family's henhouse when she was five? Because she wanted to understand where the eggs came from

What has she accomplished? Discovered that chimpanzees make and use tools

What Guinness World Record did she set? Longest-running wild primate study (Gombe Stream Chimpanzee Reserve study, which she began in 1960)

What has she said? "We're not, after all, separate from the animal kingdom. We're part of it."

What's so special about the CHIMPANZEE?

Humans share about 99 percent of their genes with chimpanzees. That makes the endangered animal our closest living relative in the animal kingdom.

SPINE-TINGLING CREATURES

Why are humans so SCARED of SHARKS?

Perhaps it's their speed in the water, pointed fins, and rows of sharp teeth? And don't forget the menacing movies about sharks on the prowl. But sharks don't hunt humans. They attack only when excited or disturbed in their territory. According to the Florida Museum of Natural History's International Shark Attack File, only ten unprovoked shark bites resulted in deaths in 2020. That said, humans kill about 100 million sharks a year, mostly in commercial fishing.

Which SNAKE is the DEADLIEST?

Probably the saw-scaled viper. Its venom isn't the strongest, but this viper kills more people each year than most other snakes combined. That might be because it is found in highly populated places. It slithers through dry areas in India, Africa, and the Middle East. The saw-scaled viper hunts at twilight and is quick to strike, with long, hinged fangs.

What is a TAPEWORM and HOW WOULD I KNOW if I had one?

You might not feel so well. But you might not have any symptoms at all. The only way you'd know for sure is seeing segments of the worm, possibly moving, in your poop. Now that's a scary animal. The tapeworm attaches to a human intestine. The long, white parasite may grow 30 feet (9 m) long inside a human. You get tapeworms by eating the undercooked meat of infected animals. Luckily, tapeworm infections are easily treated and rare in the United States.

INVADING NORTH AMERICA

Invasive species damage the environment by thriving where they are not native. These animal invaders hurt humans and the economy. Some of these species come to an area by accident. Other times, people bring them for a specific reason. Either way, invasive species are scary.

Brown Tree Snake

From Where? Australia
When Did They Arrive? 1950s
How? Arrived accidentally in Guam by stowing away on cargo ships
What Do They Do? Wipe out native birds and cause power outages by climbing wires

Burmese Python

From Where? Southeast Asia
When Did They Arrive? 2000
How? Came as pets that later escaped or were released into the wild
What Do They Do? Compete with native animals for food

Learn More

Go to National Invasive Species Information Center to find invasive species in your state.

- www.invasivespeciesinfo.gov

Cane Toad

From Where? South America
When Did They Arrive? 1930s
How? Introduced in Florida to control sugar cane pests
What Do They Do? Feed on native species and poison animals that try to bite or eat them

European Starling

From Where? Europe
When Did They Arrive? 1890
How? Introduced in New York City as a plan to bring all birds found in the works of William Shakespeare
What Do They Do? Compete with native bird species and destroy crops

OUT STANDING IN THEIR FIELD

Why do we milk mainly DAIRY COWS?

People have milked cows for thousands of years. Like humans, cows are able to produce milk only after they have given birth. A dairy cow must give birth once a year to continue providing milk. Modern farmers have bred dairy cows to produce as much as 10 gallons (38 L) of milk a day.

Why don't EGGS from the grocery store HATCH?

For an egg to hatch, it must be fertilized. To fertilize an egg, the hen and the rooster must mate before the hen lays the egg. If a hen has not mated, she lays an unfertilized egg. Most eggs from the supermarket are unfertilized eggs from a poultry farm.

Why do PIGS roll in mud?

A pig in mud is happy, as the saying goes. That's because rolling in gloppy mud helps it stay comfortably cool. Wet mud is even better than just cold water because it dries more slowly on the pig's skin. But pigs may also use mud baths to remove nasty ticks and lice from their bodies.

Make a Difference

Urge your school cafeteria to serve more vegetarian meals. Suggest meatless Mondays. Eating less meat of any kind benefits the environment.

Q&A: A Remarkable Person

Temple Grandin

Expert in Animal Behavior and Autism

When and where was she born? 1947, in Boston, Massachusetts

Why didn't she talk until she was almost four? Because she has autism spectrum disorder (ASD)

What has she accomplished? Designed a humane livestock handling system used for half of the cattle in the United States

What has she said? "Nature is cruel, but we don't have to be."

Where does she work? Professor at Colorado State University and author of numerous books on animal science and ASD

How does EATING BEEF affect the environment?

Did you know climate change and our food choices are related? Let's see how. It takes land and water to raise animals. It also takes land and water to grow food for those animals. And beef cattle require much more land than pigs or chickens do. In all, experts say one serving of red meat, like beef, produces five times as much greenhouse gas as one serving of pork or chicken. And don't forget the effects of belching. A cow's digestive system releases a large amount of methane. Cows mostly belch that dangerous gas, which also contributes to climate change. Bring on the lentil soup!

Why are BEES so important to our FOOD SUPPLY?

About one-third of the food we eat comes from crops pollinated by honey bees. That includes apples, broccoli, and almonds. There are more than 3,500 types of bees in the United States alone. After a mysterious reduction in healthy bee populations in 2006, American farmers have had to rent hives to pollinate crops.

LENDING A PAW

Why shouldn't I pet a SEEING-EYE DOG?

A harnessed seeing-eye dog means the animal is at work. Petting the dog might distract it from the job of safely guiding its handler.

Why do POLICE OFFICERS use dogs?

A highly trained police dog is known as K9 for "canine." German shepherds are the most common K9s. Patrol dogs protect officers, track suspects, and find evidence. They also locate missing people. Detection K9s are trained to uncover either drugs or explosives. Dog owners know their furry friends have a powerful sense of smell. It is 10,000 to 100,000 times more sensitive than that of a human. One scientist compared it to the ability to sniff one rotten apple in two million barrels of the fruit. There is even evidence that dogs can detect coronavirus in human sweat.

How do CAPUCHINS help people?

These clever monkeys lend a hand to people with mobility impairments. Trained capuchins can do many daily tasks. They fetch objects, turn switches, and even operate appliances. That's most impressive for a primate that weighs only about 7 pounds (3 kg).

How is a SERVICE ANIMAL different from an EMOTIONAL SUPPORT animal?

Service animals are specially trained to perform tasks for someone with a disability. That can be physical, sensory, psychiatric, or intellectual. Most official service animals are dogs. Emotional support animals may provide company, relieve loneliness, or help with depression. They don't necessarily require special training. Dogs, cats, ferrets, rabbits, parrots, pigs, even snakes can provide emotional support.

Q&A: A Remarkable Person

Judith Heumann

Activist for the Rights of People with Disabilities

When was she born and where did she grow up? 1947, in Brooklyn, New York

Why was she denied the right to attend school when she was five? Because her wheelchair was called a fire hazard

What has she accomplished? Worked to pass the Americans with Disabilities Act in 1990, which includes recognition of service animals

What has she said? "We tend to think that equality is about treating everyone the same, when it's not. It's about equity of access."

Why were CANARIES useful in coal mines?

Mining coal has always been dangerous work. In the 1910s, miners in Britain carried a caged canary to help detect toxic gases underground. If the little bird got ill or died, miners had a signal that it was time to evacuate. Carbon monoxide detectors replaced the unfortunate canaries in the 1980s.

Why do people use MINIATURE HORSES as service animals?

Although most service animals are dogs, some may be miniature horses. They must weigh less than 100 pounds (45 kg) and measure no higher than 34 inches (0.9 m). Miniature horses are easy to groom and don't cause allergies, as dogs can. And miniature horses can live more than 50 years.

PAW-SOME PETS

Why do PEOPLE have PETS?

Having a pet is an expense and a responsibility. Any pet requires proper care. Dogs demand regular walks or other exercise. They aren't your best friend for nothing! Iguanas crave heat. Gerbils are happiest in same-sex pairs. Smelly cat litter boxes need changing. Fish tanks require fresh water. Bird cages must be covered at night. But pets can increase fitness, lower stress, and bring joy to a home. That's why more than two-thirds of U.S. households own at least one pet.

Why do DOGS kick their back feet after doing their BUSINESS?

A few back kicks help mark a dog's territory. Dogs have scent glands in their feet. When they scrape the grass or dirt, the paw glands release chemicals called pheromones. It's one way of communicating to other dogs that they're in charge.

Why are some people ALLERGIC to pets?

People with pet allergies have overly sensitive immune systems. Their body reacts to proteins in the pet's pee, slobber, or dead skin flakes called dander. People may sneeze, wheeze, or cough when they are around a pet. A rash may break out. Medicine or allergy shots may provide relief. Anaphylaxis, the most severe reaction, must be treated right away.

Which PETS Are the Most POPULAR?*

TYPE OF PET	NUMBER OF HOUSEHOLDS
Dog	63.4 million
Cat	42.7 million
Freshwater fish	11.5 million
Bird	5.7 million
Small animal	5.4 million
Reptile	4.5 million

*American Pet Products Association, 2020

Make a Difference

Volunteer at a local animal shelter or rescue group. Offer to walk, feed, or clean up after the animals. You may need a parent or caregiver to go with you.

Why do CATS KNEAD?

You may have noticed cats pushing over and over against something soft with their paws. It's as if they were kneading dough. Don't worry. It's a perfectly natural activity. Cats may have learned it as kittens, kneading during nursing. Or it may be a way for them to create a soft place to rest. Kneading seems to be how cats convey comfort and happiness. Whatever the reason, you might want to keep Kitty's claws clipped.

Why are pet HAMSTERS banned in HAWAII?

The state of Hawaii is concerned about the balance of its agriculture and environment. Any hamster lover knows they are perfect escape artists! Without any natural predators, an escaped pet hamster would thrive there. Hamsters reproduce quickly and have a similar natural habitat. The banned list in Hawaii includes gerbils, geckos, toucans, and ferrets. California, New York City, and Washington, D.C., are similarly unwelcoming to ferrets.

Why can't a CHINCHILLA get wet?

A wet chinchilla takes a long time to dry. Damp fur can lead to infections. It also chills the animal, which isn't healthy. This South American rodent is a little bigger than a squirrel, with fluffy, dense fur. To keep it clean, chinchillas bathe in dust. Yes, that's right—they wash in dirt. Rolling in dust, or in fine volcanic ash from the pet store, helps remove oil from their skin.

EARTH MATTERS

Earth to readers! No matter the continent, the season, the weather, the earth is full of wonder. Oceans, bays, and corals. Rivers, lakes, and waterfalls. Lights in the night sky. Dirt in the ground. High and low spots. Erupting earth. Why are baby animals usually born in spring? Will you stay drier walking or running in the rain? What produces more of the potent gas methane: cows belching or cows farting? For answers, why on Earth would you do anything but keep reading?

SPRING INTO ACTION

Why does the AIR smell so good after a SPRING RAIN?

Two Australians researching wet weather first identified that fresh earthy scent in 1964. They named it petrichor, from the Greek *petros* ("stone") and *ichor* ("fluid that flows in veins of the gods"). Petrichor starts with a dry spell. In response, plants release oils, and bacteria in the soil produce a musky oil called geosmin. Humans are sensitive to geosmin; some can smell it when it's only five parts per trillion! Next comes the downpour. Raindrops hit plants, soil, and rocks, propelling all those oils into the air—that is petrichor you smell. You might also notice a chlorine scent before a storm. That smell is ozone, produced by lightning and other electrical discharges in the atmosphere. Humans may have evolved to appreciate these smells because we need rainwater to survive.

Why are BABY ANIMALS usually BORN in spring?

Animals most often give birth when they can easily feed themselves and their offspring. In places with snowy winters and warm summers, animals born in spring have the best chance of survival. They start life after the last snowstorms and can grow before the harsh weather of fall and winter sets in. Animals in tropical places, where food is more readily available year-round, are born in all seasons.

Q&A: A Remarkable Person

Karen Washington

Urban Farmer and Activist

When and where was she born? 1956, in New York, New York

What was her first profession? Worked as a physical therapist for more than 30 years

What did it all start with? A tomato. She said, "When I finally bit into someone's fresh, garden-grown tomato, it just changed my world. It really gave me the ambition to want to grow food myself."

What has she accomplished? Turned an empty lot in the Bronx into a community garden called the Garden of Happiness (1988), helped launch a farmers' market (1998), and cofounded Black Urban Growers to support Black farmers in the food movement (2009)

What has she said? "One thing we [Rise & Root, her farm in Chester, NY] pride ourselves on is that everyone has a right to our food, no matter what. We never turn away anyone who is hungry."

Make a Difference

Find a community garden and offer to pitch in. Or start one in your neighborhood. Or ask your family to plan one of your own. Even a small outdoor space can be used for a container garden. Prep for spring by planning what you'd like to grow and then planting new flowers or seeds.

Is SPRING FEVER an actual illness?

In the 18th century, spring fever was sometimes used as the name for scurvy, a condition caused by a lack of vitamin C. It often struck after winter, when few fresh fruits and vegetables were available in most people's diets to provide vitamin C. Scurvy results in bruises, joint swelling, and loose teeth. Today, spring fever means nothing more than a yearning for fresh air, light, and outdoor fun that comes with the end of winter.

FREE FALL

Is it AUTUMN or FALL?

The season that comes between summer and winter is called autumn. Or is it fall? Take your pick. Both words originated in Britain. The phrase "the fall of the leaves" became "fall" in the 1600s. Americans are more likely to use *fall*. *Autumn* is the more formal, older word (dates back to the 1300s).

Make a Difference

Find a public green space that needs a fall cleanup. Ask students at your school if they want to join in.

What makes LEAVES turn COLORS in the fall?

Leaves get their color from chemicals called pigments. In the spring and summer, because of a green pigment called chlorophyll, leaves are green. Chlorophyll helps absorb sunlight in the food-making process known as photosynthesis. When fall comes, it brings less daylight and cooler temperatures. It's time for leaf-shedding trees to prepare for winter. They stop growing. As their leaves lose chlorophyll, the green fades. But other pigments remain visible. Xanthophylls are responsible for the yellow colors, anthocyanins for the red colors, and carotenoids for the orange colors. (Carotenoids are also what make carrots orange.)

Why do we SWITCH OUR CLOCKS in the SPRING and FALL?

The United States first adopted daylight saving time (DST) in 1918. Contrary to popular belief, the practice has nothing to do with farming. DST was intended to save energy by decreasing the hours we need electric lights instead of sunlight. During DST, we turn the clock ahead one hour in the spring ("spring forward"). The sun rises later in the morning and sets later in the evening. We reverse the change by setting the clocks back an hour in the fall ("fall back"). DST has pros— energy saving, long summer evenings outdoors—and cons—more air conditioning, sleep loss. Guess we'll take it day by day.

What is the point of a COMPOST HEAP?

Where else can you recycle eggshells, tea bags, potato peels, apple cores, coffee grounds and filters, even hair and pet fur? Compost is organic material that can be added to soil to help plants grow. Food scraps and yard waste add up to more than 30 percent of what we throw away. Making compost with this organic material keeps it out of landfills, which take up space and release methane, a dangerous greenhouse gas.

Learn More

Go to the Herb Society of America to find out more about home composting.

- www.herbsociety.org/hsa-learn/intro-to-herbs/hsa-gardening-for-kids/composting-for-kids.html

Why are my ALLERGIES often worse in the fall?

Your nose runs, your eyes are itchy, and you can't stop sneezing. Fall triggers irritating symptoms for those allergic to ragweed, mold, and dust mites. Why at this time of year? This is when ragweed releases its pollen, which is then blown around by the wind. Mold grows in damp spots outdoors and in. That could mean in piles of wet leaves. Or in schools, where tiny pests called dust mites often thrive. *Achoo!* is right.

LET IT SNOW

Is BLACK ICE actually black?

No. That thin coating of ice just looks like the color of the paved road it forms on. Snow that melts during a sunny day often refreezes when temperatures drop in the evening. The slippery clear ice makes walking and driving extremely dangerous.

Why are AVALANCHES deadly?

Suffocation, injuries, and dangerously low body temperature (hypothermia) are the most common causes of death from avalanches. An avalanche is a mass of snow in swift motion down a mountainside. More than 150 people—mostly skiers, snowboarders, and snowmobilers—die worldwide in avalanches each year. The highest risk is 24 hours after a snowfall of 12 inches (0.3 m) or more. It takes only about five seconds for an avalanche to reach speeds of 80 miles (129 km) per hour. According to a Canadian medical journal, if one is rescued within 18 minutes, the survival rate is greater than 91 percent. Be careful out there.

Learn More

Go to Avalanche.org to see the latest conditions and accident reports.

- avalanche.org/avalanche-accidents

Can it snow when the TEMPERATURE is above FREEZING?

Believe it or not, snow has been known to fall when it's as warm as 50 degrees Fahrenheit (10 degrees Celsius). To explain: A snowflake forms when a very cold drop of water freezes around a bit of dust or pollen high in the clouds. Snowflakes usually form at or just below 32 degrees Fahrenheit (0 degrees Celsius). But rain falling continuously can cool the air around it enough to produce wet flakes.

How much snow equals an INCH OF RAIN?

You need, on average, about 13 inches (33 cm) of snow to equal 1 inch (2.5 cm) of rain. Or, if it's dry, powdery snow, you'd need almost 50 inches (127 cm). If it's sleet you're talking about, it takes only about 2 inches (5 cm) to equal 1 inch (2.5 cm) of rain.

Why do snowflakes have SIX sides?

Snowflakes are made of water molecules. A molecule is the smallest particle of any substance with the physical and chemical properties of that substance. Bonded together, water molecules take on particular shapes. It is said that they stack up like oranges in a crate, touching six other oranges, making a hexagon. Do you see the resemblance?

Q&A: A Remarkable Person

Wilson A. Bentley

Snowflake Expert

When and where was he born? 1865, in Jericho, Vermont (he died in 1931)

What did he keep a daily record of as a child? Weather conditions

How was he educated? By his mother on the family farm and in the public schools of Jericho, Vermont

What did he accomplish? Developed the science of photographing snowflakes using a camera, a microscope, and a feather (to move the snow crystals without changing their delicate form)

What else did he accomplish? Verified that snowflakes are almost always six-sided and never the same

What has he said? "Under the microscope, I found that snowflakes were miracles of beauty; and it seemed a shame that this beauty should not be seen and appreciated by others. Every crystal was a masterpiece of design and no one design was ever repeated."

IT'S A WONDER

What Are the SEVEN NATURAL WONDERS of the World?

The international news service CNN selected the following natural wonders in 1997. To be a natural wonder, a site must occur naturally, with no human intervention.

Grand Canyon

Where? Northwestern Arizona, United States
What continent? North America
Why? It's one of the world's largest and longest canyons. It is 277 miles (446 km) long, with some spots more than a mile (1.6 km) deep and 18 miles (29 km) wide.
How was it formed? By erosion (a gradual wearing away) of rock billions of years old from the Colorado River about six million years ago

Great Barrier Reef

Where? Off the northeastern coast of Australia
What continent? Australia
Why? It's the world's largest coral reef system, covering about 216,000 square miles (560,000 sq km) of the Coral Sea. It is threatened by rising sea temperatures caused by climate change.
How was it formed? By millions of corals (tiny living creatures) leaving their skeletons on which other corals grew over millions of years

Guanabara Bay

Where? Rio de Janeiro, Brazil
What continent? South America
Why? It's the world's largest natural deep-water bay (body of water partially surrounded by land).
How was it formed? By erosion from the Atlantic Ocean

Mount Everest

Where? Himalayan Mountains
What continent? Asia
Why? It's the world's tallest mountain, at 29,032 feet (8,849 m)
How was it formed? By a collision of the Indian and Eurasian tectonic plates (massive slabs of Earth's crust) some 60 million years ago

Northern Lights, or Aurora Borealis

Where? Greenland, Iceland, Norway, Canada, and United States (mostly Alaska and other northern states)
What continents? North America and Europe
Why? These natural displays of colored light appear in the Northern Hemisphere (top half of the globe) night sky, mostly in March and April and in September and October.
How do they occur? The collisions of gaseous particles with charged particles from the Sun

Parícutin Volcano

Where? Michoacán, Mexico
What continent? North America
Why? It's the world's youngest volcano, measuring 12,664 feet (3,860 m) tall.
How was it formed? From eruptions that spewed lava from 1943 to 1952

Victoria Falls

Where? Zambezi River, border of Zambia and Zimbabwe
What continent? Africa
Why? It's the world's largest waterfall, measuring more than 5,600 feet (1,700 m) across and 355 feet (108 m) high.
How much water flows over its cliff? About 33,000 cubic feet (935 cu m) of water per second

WHAT A WET ONE

Why are **FLOODS** so **DANGEROUS?**

It's easy to underestimate the power of water. Flooding can occur in every U.S. state, and floods cause more deaths each year than tornadoes, hurricanes, or lightning. Did you know it takes just 6 inches (15 cm) of fast-moving flood water to topple an adult? Only 1 foot (0.3 m) of water will float most vehicles. And 2 feet (0.6 m) of rushing water will carry a pickup truck downstream. That's why the National Weather Service advises never to drive through flooded roadways. "Turn around, don't drown!"

What is a "100-YEAR FLOOD"? Could it happen two years in a row?

A 100-year flood means there is a 1 percent chance a flood of that size will happen in any particular year. Put another way, it means a similar storm is expected to occur 1,000 times over 100,000 years, or 10,000 times over 1 million years. You get the idea. A 100-year flood two years in a row isn't likely, but it can happen.

Will you **STAY DRIER** walking or running in the rain?

Believe it or not, there is a formula to answer this.

Total wetness = (Wetness per second X Time spent in rain) + (Wetness per foot or meter X Foot or meters traveled).

Or is that too complicated? In other words, try to minimize raindrops falling on you from above by getting out of the rain as fast as possible. Run!

How LARGE can a HAILSTONE get?

The largest hailstone in the United States measured 8 inches (20.3 cm) across. It fell in Vivian, South Dakota, on July 23, 2010, weighing 1 pound, 15 ounces (0.88 kg). In the United States, Nebraska, Colorado, and Wyoming have the most hailstorms. Elsewhere, watch out for hail in China, India, Russia, Canada, and northern Italy.

What are the odds of BEING HIT BY LIGHTNING?

The odds of being hit by lightning in the United States in any year is one in 1.2 million. And you can always decrease those chances. Check weather forecasts before outdoor activities. Always go indoors during storms. Or seek shelter if you are caught out in the open. And don't ever swim if you hear thunder.

Is it possible to have THUNDER without lightning?

No. But you can spot lightning and not hear the thunder from a long distance away because the sound doesn't always carry. That's called heat lightning. Guess in which season that most often takes place? A hint: Not winter.

How Many U.S. DEATHS Are Caused by WEATHER?*

Deaths vary from year to year. These numbers are an average over 30 years.

WEATHER	DEATHS PER YEAR
Heat	143
Flood	85
Tornado	69
Hurricane	46
Lightning	39

*National Weather Service, National Oceanic Atmospheric Administration, 2020

ON ALERT

The WHYS Behind Some NATURAL EVENTS*

Natural events can cause great damage to property and the environment. They can cause injury and death. Here are some whys behind natural events that occur around the world and tips to stay safe.

Earthquake

What is it? Huge masses of rock moving beneath the earth's surface, causing the ground to shake

What causes it? Changes in the earth's outermost shell, or crust

What to do? Drop down onto your hands and knees. Cover the head and neck. Hold on to your shelter until the shaking stops.

Where is it most likely? The Ring of Fire, a belt nearly encircling the Pacific Ocean with frequent volcanic eruptions and earthquakes

Hurricane

What is it? An intense circular storm

What causes it? Warm tropical ocean air

What to do? Be prepared to remain in your home. Stay inside away from windows. Pay attention to evacuation orders.

Where is it most likely? Worldwide

Tornado

What is it? A column of rotating winds

What causes it? Spinning air currents inside the clouds of a thunderstorm

What to do? Go inside, to a basement if possible. Stay away from windows.

Where is it most likely? Central part of the United States known as the Great Plains

Rip Current

What is it? A powerful channel of fast-moving water flowing out from a shore
What causes it? Waves traveling from deep to shallow water that break near shore
What to do? Swim parallel to the shore so you can move out of the rip current.
Where is it most likely? Surf beaches around the world, including the Gulf of Mexico

Tsunami

What is it? Powerful waves caused by an underwater disturbance
What causes it? Earthquakes, sometimes volcanic eruptions or landslides
What to do? Go inland. Get to high ground. Pay attention to evacuation orders.
Where is it most likely? Active earthquake zones in the Pacific Ocean

Volcanic Eruption

What is it? An opening in the earth's crust that releases volcanic ash, hot gases, and lava
What causes it? Rapid expansion of gas bubbles inside hot liquid rock called magma, or lava once it hits the earth's surface
What to do? Go indoors. Close windows and doors. Pay attention to evacuation orders.
Where is it most likely? The Ring of Fire, a belt nearly encircling the Pacific Ocean with frequent volcanic eruptions and earthquakes

Wildfire

What is it? Uncontrolled fire in a forest or grassland
What causes it? Humans, by accident or intentionally; sometimes lightning or lava
What to do? Protect yourself from smoke. Evacuate safely.
Where is it most likely? Worldwide; most common in dry areas in the western United States, the Arctic and Siberia, Indonesia, Brazil, Argentina, and Australia

*Centers for Disease Control and Prevention, 2020

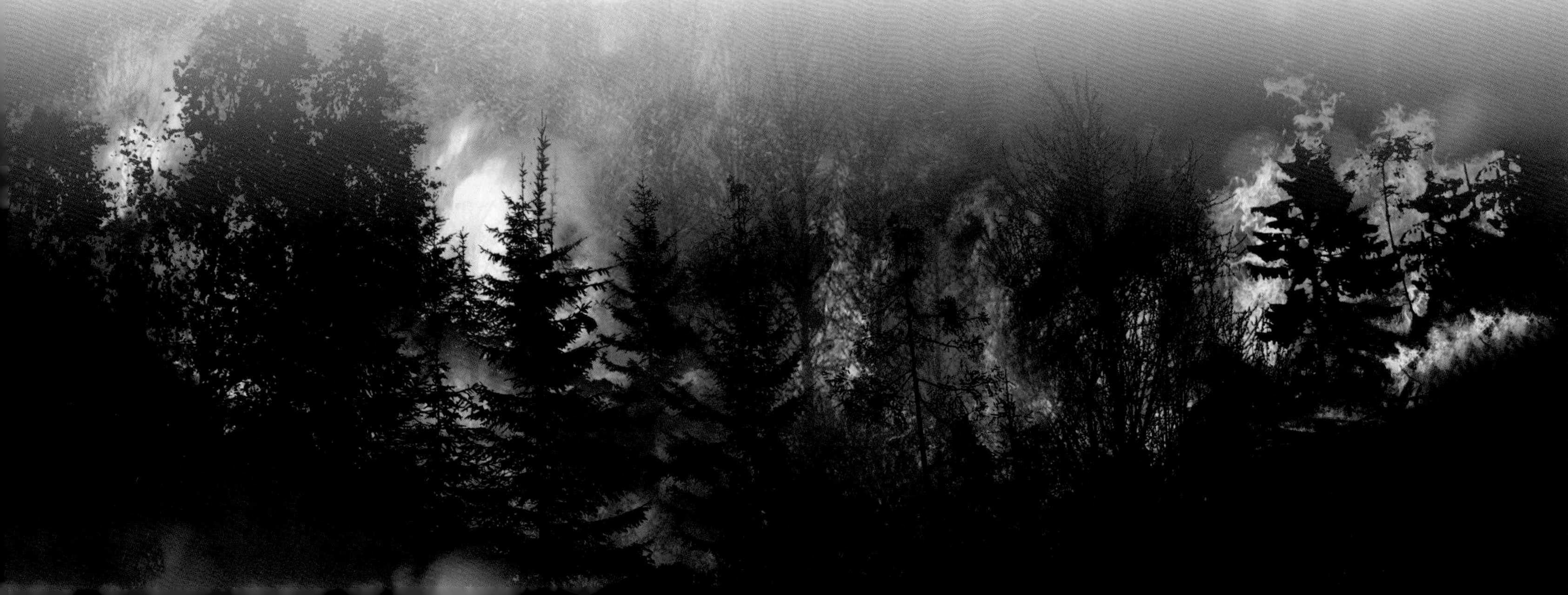

HEATING UP

What was Earth's HOTTEST MOMENT ever recorded?

On July 10, 1913, Furnace Creek Ranch, Death Valley, California, measured the highest temperature on Earth. Its official thermometer read 134 degrees Fahrenheit (56.7 degrees Celsius).

What's the difference between WEATHER and CLIMATE?

Weather is what's outside on a particular day. Climate is the average of that weather over time. Some use this expression to explain it: Climate is what you expect, weather is what you get. Climate change refers to changes over time.

How do we know the climate is CHANGING?

Scientists have observed Earth for a long time. Using satellites, weather stations, ocean buoys, and other instruments, they have collected a lot of information about the land, atmosphere, ocean, and ice. All of that information tells us that Earth's climate is getting warmer. In a recent international report, scientists predict a global average increase in Earth's temperature of 2.7 degrees Fahrenheit (1.5 degrees Celsius) could occur as early as 2040.

Why is the PLANET getting WARMER?

Humans are the main cause—mostly by burning fossil fuels such as coal, oil, and gas, which release heat-trapping, or greenhouse, gases.

Is CLIMATE CHANGE the same as GLOBAL WARMING?

No. Global warming is only a part of climate change. It refers to the long-term warming of the planet. Climate change includes the results of the warming of the atmosphere. That means rising sea levels from melting glaciers, weather patterns that produce more frequent and severe storms and droughts, and shifting seasons, all of which affect the ability of animals and plants to survive. Sometimes *global warming* is used to mean human-caused warming while *climate change* is used to mean natural warming during past ice ages.

Q&A: A Remarkable Person

Greta Thunberg

Climate Activist

When and where was she born? 2003, in Stockholm, Sweden

When was she diagnosed with autism spectrum disorder (ASD)? After she was 11; she once said, "I'm sometimes different from the norm. And—given the right circumstances—being different is a superpower."

What has she accomplished? Started Fridays for Future, a youth-led and -organized protest movement against a lack of action on the climate crisis (2018) and addressed the United Nations about climate (2019)

What does she do? Travels and strikes wherever she finds herself every Friday

What has she said? "Some people say that I should study to become a climate scientist so that I can 'solve the climate crisis.' But the climate crisis has already been solved. We already have all the facts and solutions. All we have to do is to wake up and change."

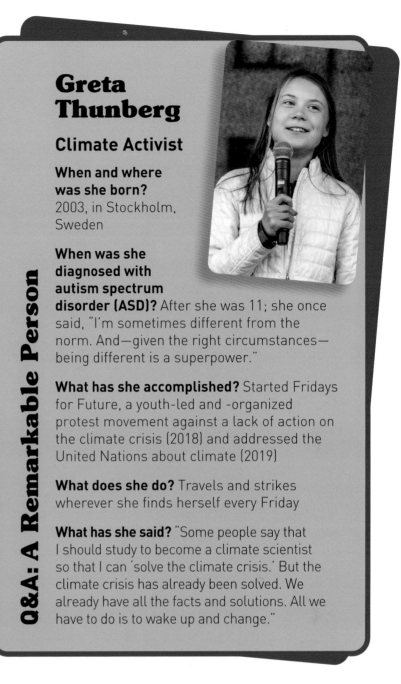

What produces more of the potent gas methane: COWS BELCHING or COWS FARTING?

Belching, by a landslide.

THE HUMAN BODY

Humans are born small and grow big. We sleep. We eat—and burp and fart! We laugh and smile. We cry. We feel nervous. We stretch and exercise our bodies. The human body has many senses and systems. Human bodies can be strong, sleepy, sad, smiley, smelly, sick, or sneezy. Why do we have eyebrows? Why do teenagers get pimples? Why does a hug make us feel better? But let's not get a-head of ourselves. Keep an eye out for on-the-nose explanations.

MAKING SENSE OF OUR SENSES

How many SENSES do I have?

Humans have five basic senses—touch, hearing, sight, smell, and taste. But there are at least four more. Knowing where your body is in space is called proprioception. This sense helps you touch your nose with your eyes closed. And kick a soccer ball without looking at your feet. Other senses relate to pain (nociception), heat (thermoception), and balance (equilibrioception). Some scientists identify as many as 53 different senses.

Why do my TEARS taste SALTY?

It's likely everyone has tasted a tear. Tears, sweat, saliva, even blood are a bit salty. Almost 1 percent of these fluids is salt. Salt helps your body work properly.

Is it true that COVID-19 can cause a loss of taste and smell?

Loss of taste and smell is a common first symptom of a COVID-19 infection. In one study, 86 percent of people with mild forms complained of loss of taste and smell. (Only about 7 percent with moderate or severe cases had the same problem.) Most patients regained their senses of taste and smell in about two months.

Why do some people gag when they taste CILANTRO?

The answer is in their family genes. They can taste a certain chemical found in cilantro—a bright green herb also known as coriander—and soap!

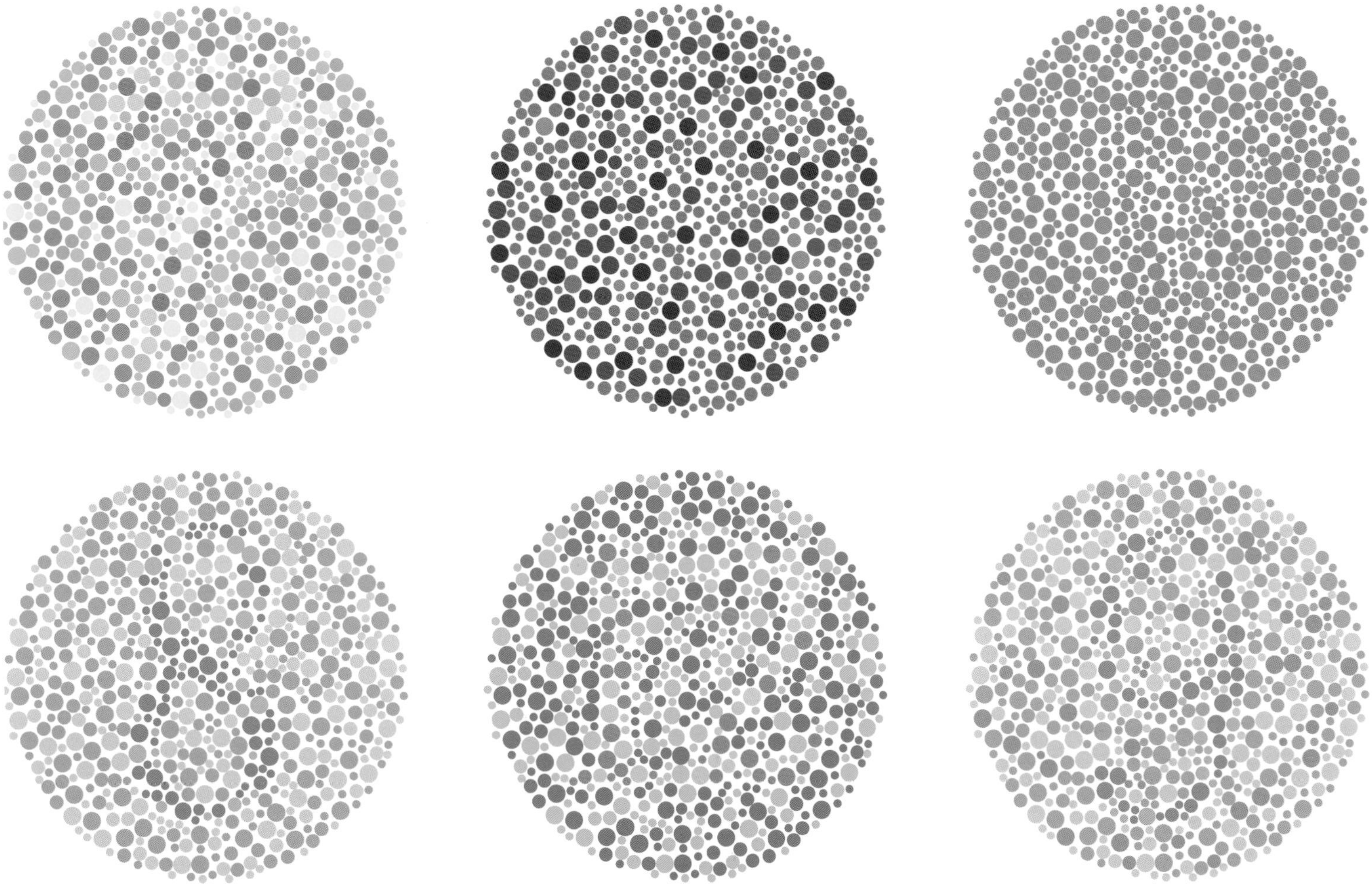

Why are some people COLOR-BLIND?

Color blindness as a rule is genetic, meaning it runs in families. If you are color-blind, you are unable to see the difference between certain colors, such as red and green or blue and green. Some people can't see any color at all, but that's unusual. Special glasses and contact lenses may help with color blindness. Men are more likely to be color-blind—as many as 1 in 12 of them have the condition.

Is it safe to listen to MUSIC using EARBUDS?

Loud sounds over extended periods can damage hearing. When it comes to earbuds, doctors often recommend using them for no more than 60 minutes at a time at no more than 60 percent of the maximum volume. Another tip to stay safe when you're out and about with headphones is making sure you can hear the cars, bicycles, and other activity around you.

Why does a HUG from a LOVED ONE make me feel better?

A hug is one of the ways we give and receive emotional support. A welcome touch is a powerful way to share feelings. Hugs release the hormone oxytocin, which can lift your mood and even ward off illness by lowering stress. A bear hug from a loved one when you're feeling down is the best.

WHY DO I DO THAT?

Why do I SNEEZE?

A sneeze can be your best friend. Hey, it protects you from bacteria and bugs! When germs—or dust or pollen or smoke—enter your nose, they interact with the tiny hairs and sensitive skin lining it. Your body responds by sneezing to clear your nasal passages. But sneezing can also spread viruses, such as the flu and coronavirus, in droplets of saliva. That's why it's best to cover your mouth when you sneeze.

Why do I YAWN?

You yawn when you're tired or just waking up. But boredom, anxiety, and hunger also bring on yawns. One theory is that yawning—taking a deep breath and stretching your jaw—increases blood flow to your skull. That helps cool the brain, which is useful in keeping you alert. Did you know that seeing a yawn will make most people yawn within five minutes? Perhaps yawning evolved as a way to keep groups awake and prepared.

Why do I HICCUP?

Eating or drinking too quickly sometimes causes hiccups. Hiccups are contractions of the diaphragm, the muscle below your lungs. It's the sudden closing of your vocal cords that produce the "hiccup" sound. Hiccups are a reflex—you have no control over them. Holding your breath can help break the rhythm of the spasms, which usually don't last more than a few minutes. Unless you're Charles Osborne. He hiccupped for 68 years until they suddenly stopped a year before he died at age 96.

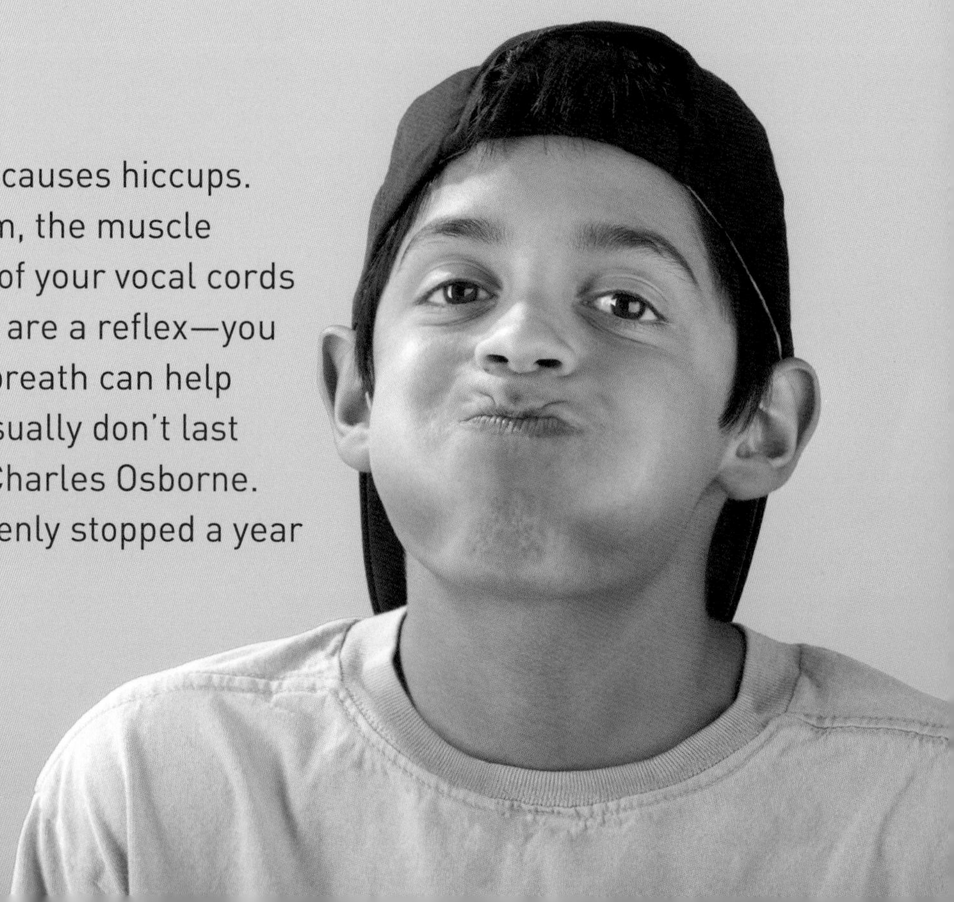

Q&A: A Remarkable Person

Michael Phelps

Most Decorated Olympic Athlete

When and where was he born? 1985, in Baltimore, Maryland

When was he diagnosed with ADHD? In sixth grade, the same year he swam three hours at the pool every day after school

What record did he set? The most medals in Olympic history (23 gold, 3 silver, and 2 bronze)

What else has he accomplished? Founded a charity that promotes healthy, active lives, especially for children, primarily through the sport of swimming

What has he said? "Things won't go perfect. It's all about how you adapt from those things and learn from mistakes."

Why do I FAINT? (What is fainting?)

Standing up too quickly can sometimes cause fainting, or passing out briefly from a lack of oxygen to the brain. It could also be a sign of hunger, anxiety, pain, or heat exhaustion. Or just dehydration, a lack of water in your body. Fainting is not necessarily a sign of serious illness. If you ever feel lightheaded or dizzy, lie with your legs raised or sit, head between your knees. Or else drink water, eat something, and breathe slowly.

Why do kids FIDGET?

Everyone struggles to concentrate—and probably fidgets—sometimes. Research says fidgeting can make the brains of some people more focused. Millions of kids and adults have Attention-Deficit Hyperactivity Disorder (ADHD), which can make them daydreamy or unusually active, or fidgety. ADHD is caused by differences in the brain, not being lazy or undisciplined.

FOOD FOR THOUGHT

Is it true "an APPLE a day keeps the doctor away"?

Eating more apples doesn't necessarily mean fewer visits to the doctor, according to research. However, apples are nutritious, good for your heart, and may reduce the risk of cancer. You can take it to heart—medical professionals agree eating fruit and vegetables is part of a healthy diet.

Why does SPICY FOOD make me sweat?

Your nose is running, your eyes are watering, your face is flushed, and you're sweating. No, you're not sick, you just bit into a hot pepper. The main ingredient in a hot pepper is called capsaicin. When you eat it, your body sweats, as if in a hot environment. Oh, and drinking water does nothing to relieve the burn. Capsaicin isn't soluble in water. The best thing to do is drink milk, which has fat in it that helps dissolve the capsaicin.

Why does JUNK FOOD taste so delicious?

Artificial food coloring and flavors, high-fructose corn syrup, and trans fats can make junk food appealing to look at, smell, and eat. But most junk food is highly processed, meaning it is far from its natural state. Think high-sugar breakfast cereals or fruit snacks and high-salt chips. All are high in calories and low in nutrients. Like many things, junk food is best in moderation.

Why is it called BREAKFAST?

Fasting is going without food. When you scramble your eggs or pour your cereal, you are breaking the fast you started when you went to sleep the previous night. That's why it's called breakfast. People have eaten a morning meal since ancient times. They used the word *breakfast* for the first time in the 15th century.

Could I outgrow a FOOD ALLERGY?

Yes. About 10 percent of two-year-olds—and 7 percent of children aged 14 to 17—have serious allergies to food. Young people often outgrow their allergies to milk, eggs, wheat, and soy. But outgrowing allergies to peanuts, tree nuts, fish, shrimp, and sesame is unusual. On the not-so-bright side, you can develop a new food allergy at any age.

THE WHYS BEHIND HEALTHY EATING

To run smoothly, the human body needs nourishing food. Here are the whys behind some suggestions for healthy eating.

Rethink Your Drink

How? Drink fat-free or low-fat milk or water instead of sugary drinks.
Why? Sugar causes tooth decay.

Eat More Fruits and Veggies

How? Make half your plate fruits and vegetables every day.
Why? Fruits and vegetables provide the vitamins and nutrients your body needs. They also fill you up in a healthy way.

Slow Down on Sweets

How? Eat sweets once in a while in small amounts.
Why? Tooth decay (again!)

Choose Whole Grains

How? Try oatmeal, whole-wheat breads, or brown rice at meals.
Why? Grains are high in fiber, which fill you up in a healthy way. Whole grains can also lower risk for some diseases.

Focus on Lean Protein

How? Choose beans, fish, lean meats, and nuts.
Why? Eating protein low in fat helps you build muscle in a healthy way.

LET'S SLEEP ON IT

Why do BABIES SLEEP so much?

Newborn babies need as much as 18 hours of sleep in a 24-hour period. When they aren't asleep, they're eating up to 12 times a day. That's a lot of dirty diapers. But all that eating and sleeping helps a baby grow physically. It's mostly during deep sleep that a hormone that spurs growth is released. Sleeping also helps a baby's brain develop. Sleep on, baby!

What makes people SNORE?

Snoring is common—and loud. It can be caused by allergies, asthma, or large tonsils. Snorers sleep with their mouths open. Tissues at the back of the throat vibrate with each breath, producing noises ranging from a quiet whistle to a jackhammer. One quarter of children snore now and then. The same fraction of adults snores regularly. And it can worsen with age. Sleeping on your side helps reduce snoring. Some snorers have sleep apnea, a disorder in which breathing stops repeatedly. Treatment involves the use of a machine that gently blows pressurized air through the nose to keep the airway open during sleep.

How Much SLEEP Do Kids Need a Day?*

AGE	NUMBER OF HOURS
4 to 12 months	12 to 16 (incl. naps)
1 to 2 years	11 to 14 (incl. naps)
3 to 5 years	10 to 13 (incl. naps)
6 to 12 years	9 to 12
13 to 18 years	8 to 10

*American Academy of Sleep Medicine, 2016

Why do people have SOMNAMBULISM? (What is somnambulism?)

If you knew the Latin words *somnum* ("sleep") and *ambulare* ("to walk"), could you guess the answer? That's right—sleepwalking. Sleepwalkers might get out of bed, walk, talk, or eat while mostly asleep and not remember it in the morning. Episodes start during deep sleep. They usually last from 5 to 15 minutes. Sleepwalking is often passed through families (almost half of young sleepwalkers have a parent who sleepwalked as a child). A lack of sleep, illness, or stress can lead to the disorder. Sleepwalking is far more common in children than in adults, and teenagers often outgrow it.

Can using my PHONE or TABLET before bed affect my sleep?

Yup! Did you know electronic devices give off a blue light? This blue light suppresses the production of melatonin, a hormone related to sleep cycles. Looking at your smartphone keeps your mind active and engaged, which isn't calming before bed. Sleep experts recommend putting your phone away 30 to 60 minutes before bed.

Why do TEENAGERS want to sleep so late?

Well, they might be tired from homework, activities, jobs, and hanging out with friends. But there could be a scientific explanation. The internal clock resets during adolescence, telling teens to fall asleep later and wake up later. At about 10:30 p.m. every night, older teens produce melatonin, which helps them fall asleep. (That happens about one hour earlier for younger teens.) This is why many school boards, pediatricians, and families have been calling for later school start times for middle- and high-school students. Everyone needs their Z's to thrive.

DON'T SWEAT IT

Why do I sweat when I EXERCISE?

When exercising or other activities make you feel hot, sweating cools your body down. Your brain responds to the heat by releasing sweat through tiny holes called pores. Drops of sweat evaporate, cooling the skin and releasing heat, which helps return your body temperature to normal. That's why drinking fluids during your sweat sesh, especially on hot days, is so important—to replace the water you've lost.

Why does sweat STINK?

Pure sweat actually doesn't smell. But when the bacteria that lives on your skin mixes with sweat from the glands in your armpits, the smell can be, well, stinky.

How much exercise do KIDS need?

At least 60 minutes of activity every day for kids aged 6 to 17, according to the U.S. Department of Health and Human Services. It doesn't have to be all at once. Walking to school or the bus in the morning, playing an active game at the park in the afternoon, and taking your dog out in the evening all count toward the total.

How do you stop a NOSEBLEED on the sports field?

No one likes the sight of blood, especially your own, but it's not so hard to stop a nosebleed. Sit up or stand, lean forward, and pinch your nostrils closed for 10 minutes. It can feel like a long time. Don't forget to breathe through your mouth. Applying pressure to the bleeding point in this way should stop the flow of blood. Play on!

How do CASTS heal broken bones?

Breaking a bone is possible in almost any sport. Casts work to hold the broken bone in place. The body heals itself naturally. Of course, that's after a doctor has examined an X-ray and set the bone (lined it in the proper position).

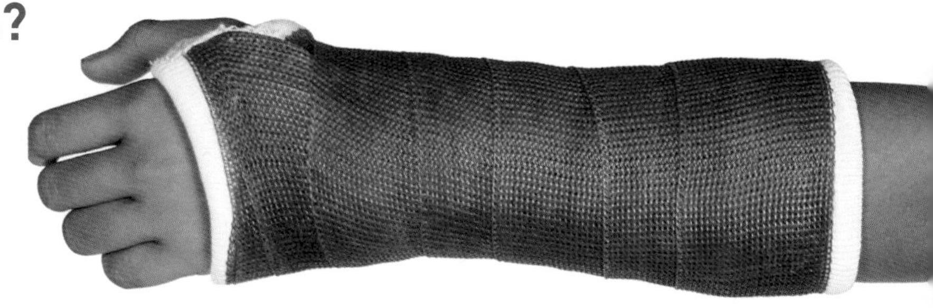

THE WHYS BEHIND SPORTS SAFETY*

To stay healthy, the human body needs to stretch, exercise, and recover. Here are the whys behind some sports safety tips.

Warm Up

How? Stretch to release muscle tension.
Why? Stretching before activity keeps your muscles flexible, strong, and healthy.

Hydrate

How? Drink water 30 minutes before activity and every 20 minutes during activity.
Why? Water prevents you from getting muscle cramps, feeling faint, and collapsing from heatstroke.

Make a Difference

Organize a sweat sesh with the family or a group of friends. Go for a nature walk or plan an outdoor game. Being active strengthens your muscles—including your heart!—and bones. Did you know exercise can even improve your mood?

Choose the Right Gear

How? Find and use the proper helmet, shin guards, mouthguards, pads, eye protection, and footwear.
Why? Equipment that doesn't fit you properly or is made for a different sport can cause injury.

Don't Take Chances with the Brain—or the Rest of Your Body

How? Recover from all injuries fully, including a concussion (a type of injury to the brain).
Why? Returning to play too soon increases the risk of another and perhaps more serious injury. When in doubt, sit it out!

*Safe Kids Worldwide, 2021

EMOTIONS IN MOTION

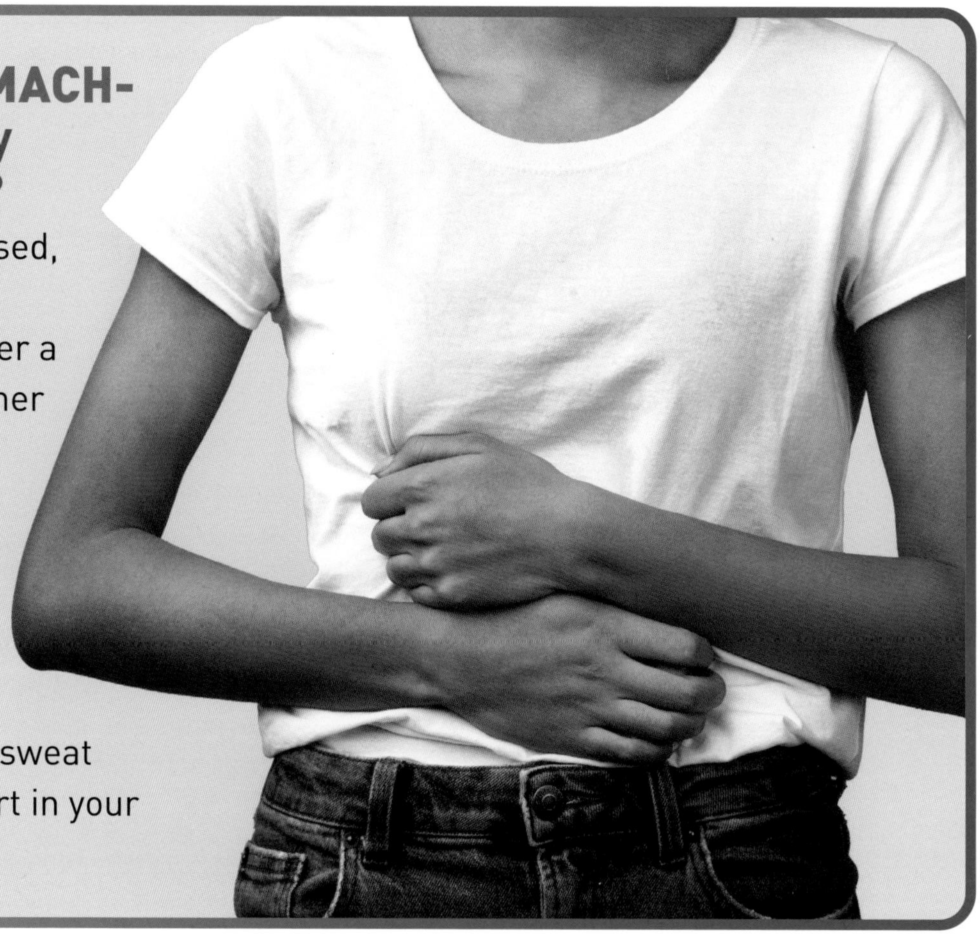

Why do I have a STOMACH-ACHE and get sweaty when I'm NERVOUS?

When you're scared or stressed, your body enters a "fight-or-flight" survival response. After a release of adrenaline and other hormones, your heart races, you breathe more rapidly, your blood flow increases, and your muscles tense. You are ready to react to a threat. But the adrenaline rush has also activated your sweat glands and caused discomfort in your belly. It's time to chill out!

Why do people tell me to TAKE A DEEP BREATH when I'm upset?

Filling your lungs with oxygen is one of the best ways to lower stress in your body. It also helps cool your emotions by giving you something to focus on. While telling someone to calm down usually has the opposite effect, suggesting a deep breath might work.

Make a Difference

Breathe in slowly through your nose. Then exhale slowly through your mouth. Repeat it two times. Do you notice a change in how you feel? Ask a sibling or friend to try it with you.

Will FAKING A SMILE make me feel better?

Forcing it may actually improve your mood. In a recent study, participants were asked to hold a pen in their teeth, which uses the same facial muscles as a smile. Researchers found it triggered the same brain chemicals as a genuine smile. Participants apparently saw the world around them in a more positive way. Fakery is not a way of life, but if you're feeling a bit blue, give it a try!

Why LAUGH?

Everyone likes a funny joke. Our earliest giggles can come three months into life. Laughter may have evolved as a way to connect with others. Want proof? People laugh an average of 18 times a day. We are 30 times more likely to laugh in a group than alone. (Research also shows that about 80 percent of the time people respond with laughter to things that aren't funny at all.) A belly laugh is healthy for the body. Cracking up increases your intake of oxygen, releases feel-good chemicals called endorphins, and relieves stress.

Why do I feel better after A GOOD CRY?

Humans are the only animals who cry for emotional reasons. Like a laugh, a good cry is both a way to communicate and a release of stress (and endorphins, those feel-good chemicals your body produces naturally). When you're happy or sad or in pain, you shed emotional tears. These drops even contain a natural painkiller produced when you experience stress. All of that might be why you often feel better after a sob session.

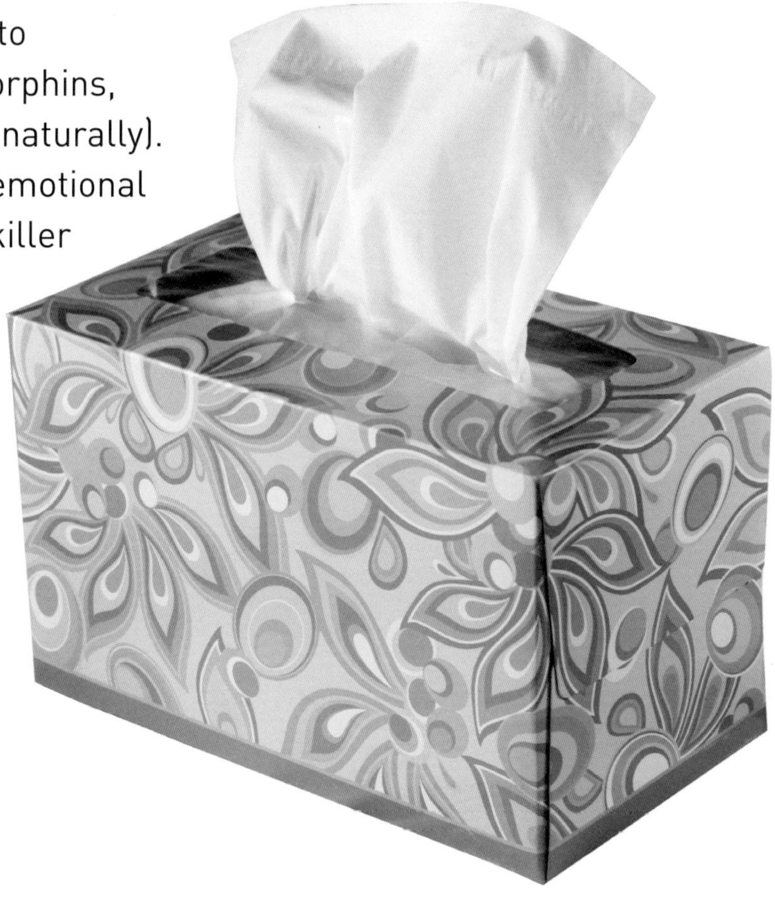

Learn More

Go to Mindful to find a three-minute meditation for kids.

- www.mindful.org/mindfulness-for-kids

GET THE SKINNY

Why is my **THUMBPRINT** unique?

Little ridges on fingertips begin to form in the womb. They begin to develop their own patterns of arches, loops, and whorls after three months. Fingerprints don't change as you age. The chances of your fingerprint matching exactly with anyone else's is one in 64 billion. Even identical twins don't have the same ones.

Why do teenagers get **PIMPLES**?

With the teenage years often come pimples. They're also called zits, blackheads, whiteheads, or acne. During this time of life, the skin produces extra oil that sometimes clogs the pores. That oil combines with dead skin and bacteria to form small inflammations, or pimples. More than 80 percent of teens have acne. Popping a zit isn't recommended. It can further irritate the skin, causing swelling, redness, and even a scar. It's better to wash with a gentle cleanser and wait it out, or use a drying gel or cream from the drugstore.

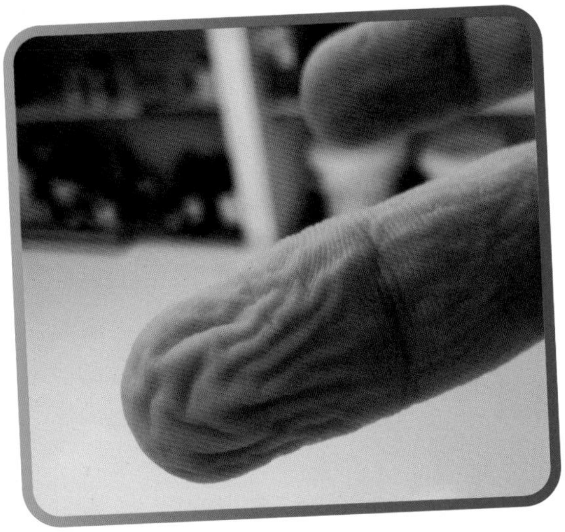

Why do my **FINGERTIPS** get **WRINKLY** in water?

The outermost layer of your skin is covered with a special oil called sebum. Sebum helps prevent loss of moisture. It's a kind of waterproofing for your body. Being in a pool or the bathtub for a time washes sebum away, and your skin becomes waterlogged. But don't worry, as you have probably noticed, these water wrinkles don't remain long. Once the water has dried up and more sebum is produced, your fingertips are back to normal.

Why do people get **WRINKLES** when they get **OLDER**?

As you age, the skin becomes less elastic and more fragile. The weight of the skin can cause it to sag. Wrinkles are just a part of the glory of long life.

What causes **FRECKLES?**

Freckles are caused by a combination of your family's genes and exposure to the sun. People with freckles are mostly likely to have skin and eyes that are light in color. Freckles appear after the age of five and often fade in adults.

What's wrong with TANNING?

For starters, if you end up with a sunburn, it can hurt. Red, swollen, sometimes blistered skin can be quite painful. Then, after the burn fades, or peels off, your skin has suffered lasting damage. Ultraviolet (UV) radiation from the sun ages the skin prematurely and over time increases risk of certain diseases. Not all sun damage is visible. But the good news is it's easy to prevent. Use plenty of sunscreen. Wear a hat, sunglasses, and protective clothing when you're out in the sun.

Learn More

Go to the Centers for Disease Control and Prevention to find some success stories about sun safety.

- www.cdc.gov/cancer/skin/success-stories

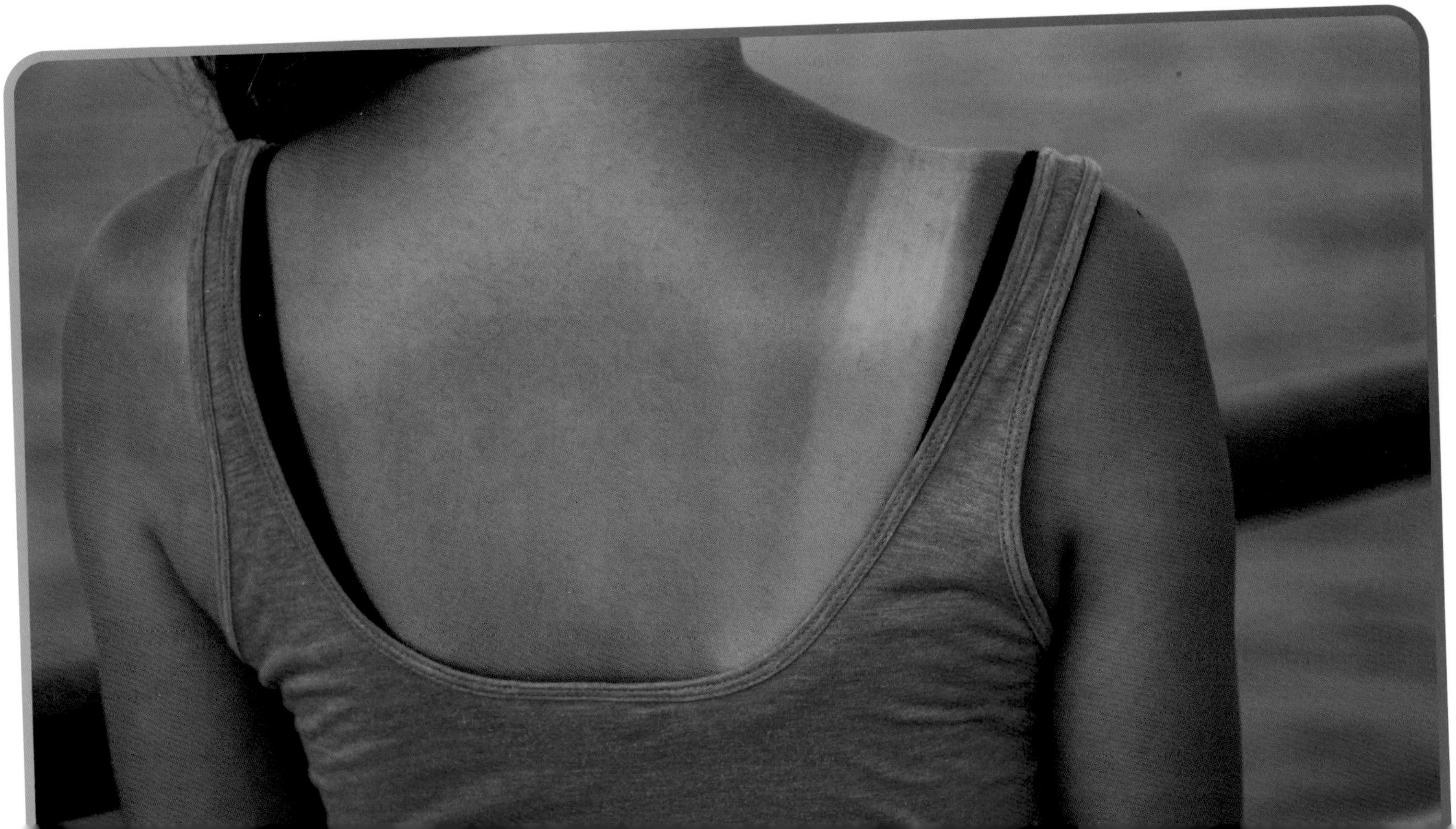

TOUGH AS NAILS AND HAIR

Why do I have EYEBROWS?

Eyebrows, and eyelashes, for that matter, protect your eyes from water and sunlight. The arches of hair channel sweat and rainwater dripping down your forehead away from your eyes. But eyebrows also help you connect and communicate with those around you. Eyebrows tell others how you are feeling. They go up slightly to convey happiness, pull together to express pity, and raise the highest to show surprise or fear. That's impressive for two little strips of hair on your face.

How FAST does my HAIR GROW?

Hair on the scalp grows about 6 inches (15 cm) a year. The average head has about 100,00 hairs. As many as 150 of them fall out every day. Your hair is always growing, resting, falling out, and replacing itself. You know what they say—hair today, gone tomorrow!

Why do some men go BALD?

Most bald men lose their hair because of androgenetic alopecia. This condition, also called male-pattern baldness, is passed through families. About 25 percent of men with male-pattern baldness start losing their hair before age 21. But nearly everyone, with age, experiences some hair loss.

Make a Difference

There are organizations that provide free wigs and other hairpieces to young people living with hair loss. Consider making a hair donation.

Why do we have FINGERNAILS?

Your nails—and hair and skin—are made of a tough protein called keratin. Keratin is also found in the fur, horns, and claws of animals. Nails, a flatter, wider form of claws, protect the tips of the fingers and toes. They also aided past humans in picking up, tearing, and grasping objects like food.

How fast do my FINGERNAILS GROW?

Human fingernails grow about 1 inch (3 cm) a year. Their rate of growth is faster in the summer than the winter. For unknown reasons, fingernails tend to grow faster on the hand you write with. Also, fingernails grow about three times faster than toenails. All of your nails grow more slowly as you age.

Why do some people BITE their nails?

Nail biting can be a sign of anxiety or boredom. Or hunger. (Yikes!) It's often something people do without thinking. The repetitive action can be soothing. Biting nails seems to be genetic in part. Kids with parents who bite their nails are more likely to be nail biters.

What makes hair turn WHITE?

Hair gets its color from a pigment called melanin. Lighter hair has less melanin, and darker hair has more melanin. As people age, their hair follicles produce less melanin, and their hair color becomes lighter. It eventually looks gray, or white. Many people rock a silver mane.

GROSS, JUST GROSS

Why do my **FEET REEK** by the end of the day?

Bacteria eat the dead skin and oils on your feet. When they get warm and moist in your shoes after a long day, the bacteria grow, releasing a smell some people have compared to cheese. With good reason! It's the same bacteria used to ripen certain cheeses. Wash (and dry) your feet regularly. Give your footwear a few days off to dry out, and always wear fresh socks to help absorb the sweat.

What are **BOOGERS?**

Boogers are dried pieces of nasal mucus, also known as snot. They keep the inside of your nose from drying out and warm the air you breathe. They also prevent dust, pollen, and viruses from entering your lungs.

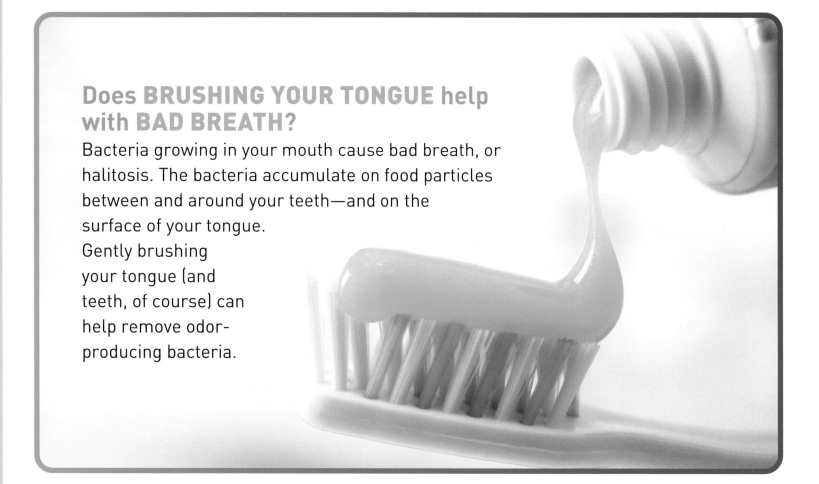

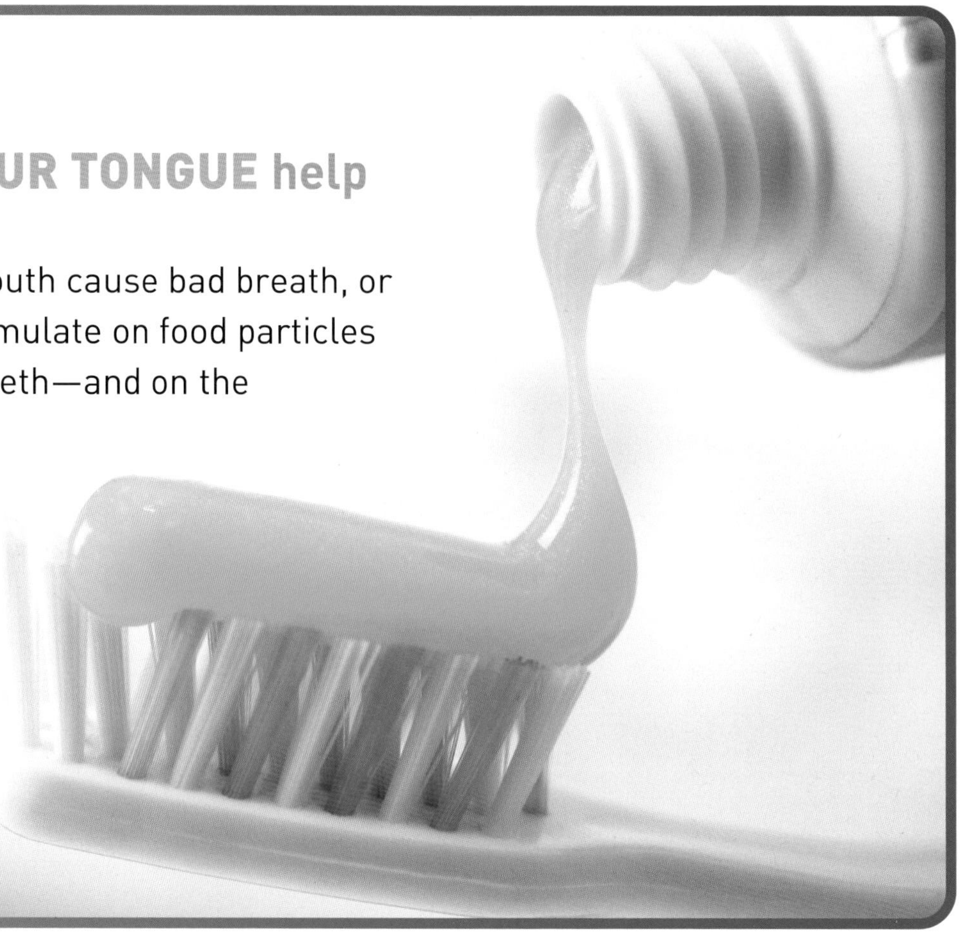

Does **BRUSHING YOUR TONGUE** help with **BAD BREATH?**

Bacteria growing in your mouth cause bad breath, or halitosis. The bacteria accumulate on food particles between and around your teeth—and on the surface of your tongue. Gently brushing your tongue (and teeth, of course) can help remove odor-producing bacteria.

What causes CRUSTY EYES in the morning?

Healthy eyes produce mucus, which keeps them moist and clean. During the day, blinking naturally washes it away. Because we don't blink when we're asleep, this mucus can collect in the corner of our eyes, where it dries out.

Why is pee sometimes a LIGHTER YELLOW?

The more water you drink, the lighter the color of your pee. Lighter yellow urine means you are well hydrated. Keep it up!

What makes people FART AND BURP?

We burp to get rid of the air we take in, usually while eating or drinking. As much as 1 tablespoon (15 ml) of air can enter your stomach each time you swallow. We fart because of a buildup of gas in the body, also caused by eating and drinking. The process of digesting food produces additional gas. Just remember to say excuse me.

Why do I have WAX in my EARS?

Ear wax serves a useful purpose. It moisturizes your ear canal, prevents infection, and keeps your ear clear of dust and dirt. Did you hear that?

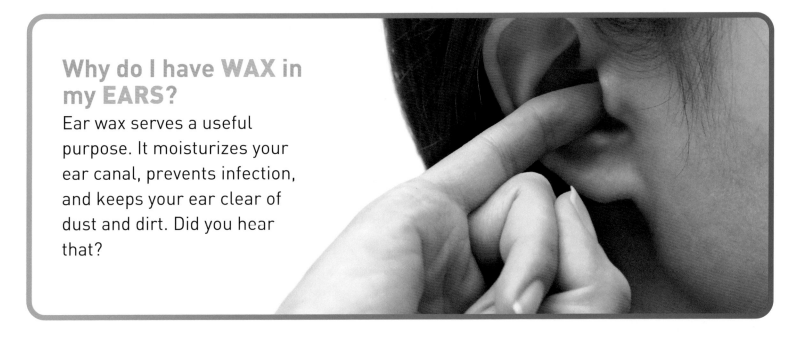

Why does POOP stink?

The smell comes from bacteria that live in your gut. They help break down the food you eat. In the process, they emit gases not always pleasant to the senses. It's perfectly normal to have stinky poop. And for the smell to vary based on what you ate. Perhaps we'll just leave it at that.

NATIONS AND PEOPLE

The world's nations and people are amazing and varied. So are the structures we build and the things we create. The languages we speak. The places we live. The history we make. The figures who lead us. Why did people draw on cave walls? Are there any global words? Why do countries change their names? What do all human beings have in common? Keep reading for global answers.

THE REST IS (PRE) HISTORY

When did PREHISTORY start?

A long time ago. Millions of years ago. Prehistory is the name for all of the years before humans began to write.

If there is NO WRITTEN RECORD of prehistory, how do we know it happened?

Almost all we know about prehistoric life comes from physical evidence of ancient cities and other sites, much of it discovered by scientific digs. At a dig, archaeologists uncover objects and structures that were made, used, and left behind by humans. Studying these prehistoric artifacts can provide much information about the past.

How can SCIENTISTS be sure of the age of prehistoric ARTIFACTS?

Carbon dating is one way to determine the age of an artifact. All living plants and animals contain some natural radioactive carbon-14. (Don't worry. It isn't harmful to people.) After a plant or animal dies, the carbon-14 slowly decays. That decay can be measured and used to estimate how old an object is. Wood, seeds, hair, leather, shells, even pigments in wall paintings can be carbon dated.

Why did people draw on CAVE WALLS?

Early humans communicated with signs, gestures, and likely some form of speech. But before written language or sound recording devices, we can't know much about their communications firsthand! Pictures or carved images in rock are actual lasting evidence we have of humans expressing themselves tens of thousands of years ago. Are these images storytelling or recordkeeping or information sharing or a form of art? It's hard to know. Many of the oldest examples were discovered in caves, where they were protected from elements that could have erased them. Archaeologists in Indonesia recently found what may be the world's oldest cave art. One painting of an awesome life-sized wild pig is estimated to be at least 45,000 years old. The artist also created a dark red outline of two handprints. Delicate paintings of horses, lions, and reindeer were discovered in France's Chauvet cave in 1994. They date back "only" about 35,000 years.

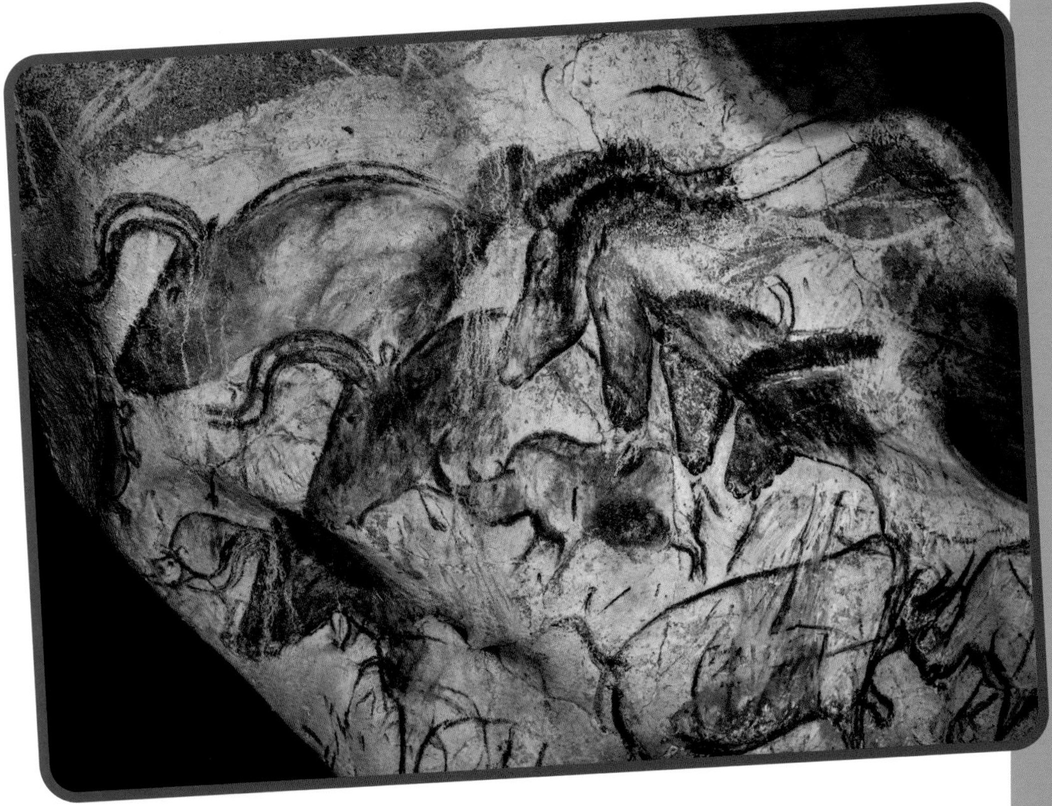

Q&A: A Remarkable Person

Mary Leakey

Archaeologist

When and where was she born? 1913, in London, England (she died in 1996)

When did she first work at a dig in England? When she was 17, beginning as an illustrator

What did she accomplish? Found several fossils (remains of ancient life), including of a skull more than 18 million years old (1948), that furthered scientific understanding of the origins of humans

What else did she accomplish? In 1978, at a site in northern Tanzania, discovered fossilized footprints of human ancestors that seemed to prove they walked on two legs earlier than previously believed

What did she say? "There is so much we do not know, and the more we do know, the more we realize that early interpretations were completely wrong."

MAKING HISTORY

Why is it called the **STONE AGE?** (And what is the Stone Age?)

The time in prehistory when humans made stone tools is called the Stone Age. The earliest human tools—from more than 3 million years ago—were made of stone. They were also made of wood, animal skins, and plant fibers, but those materials didn't survive. So "Stone Age" it is.

When did **RECORDED HISTORY** start?

History started more than 5,000 years ago, when the Sumerians of Mesopotamia invented a writing system. Archaeologists discovered clay tablets with markings called cuneiform in today's Iraq that prove it. They also discovered written records from 3200 BCE in Egypt. That writing system is called hieroglyphics, or "holy carvings." Prehistory was history.

Make a Difference

Set up an interview with an older family member about their personal recollections of the past. Or ask them about a tradition or recipe from their culture. Consider making a recording, video, or written record to share with your family, class, or library. This way of preserving historical information is called oral history.

Does history actually **REPEAT** itself?

It depends on your perspective. Some historians say it can be helpful to look at the past to predict the future. The more things change, the more they stay the same, as the expression goes. Other historians say studying recent events provides better clues about what lies ahead. Either way, we learn from studying history, recent or long past.

Why do we use BCE and CE?

BCE stands for "Before Common Era" (before the birth of Jesus). CE stands for "Common Era." These terms are now often used instead of BC ("Before Christ") and AD (*anno Domini*, Latin for "in the year of the lord"). Using BC and AD ties the world's vast historical calendar to only one religion—Christianity.

Why is there a little *c* before some OLD DATES?

That *c* is short for "circa," from the Latin for "around." Historians use this little *c* before any date that is uncertain. The Mongol emperor from central Asia, Genghis Khan, for example, was born c. 1155. Or c. 1162. Or maybe c. 1167.

What Have We LEARNED and Made THROUGH THE AGES?*

Since the Stone Age, we humans have "built" on our knowledge and discovered new materials. That knowledge and those materials have allowed us to build and create the world around us.

AGE	SPAN OF TIME	WHAT HUMANS DID WITH THE MATERIAL
Stone	More than 3 million years ago to 3200 BCE	Made stone tools for hunting, food preparation, and defense
Bronze	3200 BCE to 1200 BCE	Melted copper and tin together to cast better tools and weapons
Iron	1200 BCE to 100 CE	Crafted stronger and lighter weapons, chains, and farm tools
Glass	1300 to present	Produced transparent windows, bottles, and lenses
Steel	1800s to present	Built skyscrapers, railroads, arms, and silverware
Plastic	1907 to present	Used it to mold almost anything, though it is a pollutant

*Institution of Engineering and Technology, 2019

AROUND THE WORLD WONDERS

What Are Today's SEVEN WONDERS of the World?

A Swiss foundation organized a public online survey in 2000 to select the following historic structures. All of the selected sites are also United Nations Educational, Scientific and Cultural Organization (UNESCO) World Heritage Sites.

Chichén Itzá

Where? Yucatán state, Mexico
What continent? North America
Why? It's a ruined ancient city of the Maya tribe called the Itzá. The tallest structure is a pyramid, 79 feet (24 m) high, with as many steps as there are days in a year—365.
When was it built? In the sixth century

Colosseum

Where? Rome, Italy
What continent? Europe
Why? It's the largest ancient amphitheater ever built. It once held 50,000 people, who gathered to watch gladiators battle.
When was it built? In the first century

Christ the Redeemer

Where? Rio de Janeiro, Brazil
What continent? South America
Why? It's a huge, streamlined statue of Jesus Christ, the central figure of Christianity, built on a mountain peak out of concrete and covered in millions of tiles. The landmark is 98 feet (30 m) tall; the outstretched arms measure 92 feet (28 m) across.
When was it built? 1926 to 1931

Great Wall of China

Where? Northern China and southern Mongolia
What continent? Asia
Why? Its numerous walls make up one of the world's largest human-made structures. Built to keep out invading armies, the dirt, stone, and brick wall measures more than 5,000 miles (8,000 km) long.
When was it built? Begun in the seventh century BCE

Machu Picchu

Where? Andes Mountains, Peru
What continent? South America
Why? It's the ruins of an Inca city, with plazas, temples, and thousands of stone steps. *Machu picchu*, or "old peak" in the Inca language Quechua, stands at a height of 7,710 feet (2,350 m).
When was it built? From mid-1400s to mid-1500s

Petra

Where? Southwestern Jordan
What continent? Asia
Why? It's an ancient Arab city, with tombs, an innovative water system, and buildings carved into sandstone cliffs. Petra, which comes from "rock" in Greek, was formerly occupied by Nabataeans, ancient Romans, and then Muslims.
When was it built? As early as the fourth century BCE

Taj Mahal

Where? Agra, India
What continent? Asia
Why? It's the world's foremost example of Mughal architecture, a combination of Indian, Persian, and Islamic styles. The white marble structure, with a central dome 240 feet (73 m) high, honored a Mughal emperor's wife, who died in childbirth.
When was it built? From about 1632 to 1648

JUST HOW MANY?

How many **CONTINENTS** are there?

Earth has seven major land masses called continents. They are, from biggest to smallest: Asia, Africa, North America, South America, Antarctica, Europe, and Australia. Europe and Asia are sometimes considered one continent—Eurasia. By that count, there are only six continents. But you knew that.

How many people live in **ANTARCTICA?**

Zero. Antarctica has no permanent residents. Perhaps that is because this southernmost continent is also the coldest. Antarctica isn't a country, and it has no government. But it is huge in territory, covering about 5.5 million square miles (14.2 million sq km). The land is almost entirely an ice sheet. The weather is dry and windy. In 1959, 12 nations signed the Antarctic Treaty. They agreed to use the continent only for peaceful, scientific purposes. Now that number is 54 and includes the United States, Russia, and China. Antarctica is home to numerous research stations, staffed by people from around the world.

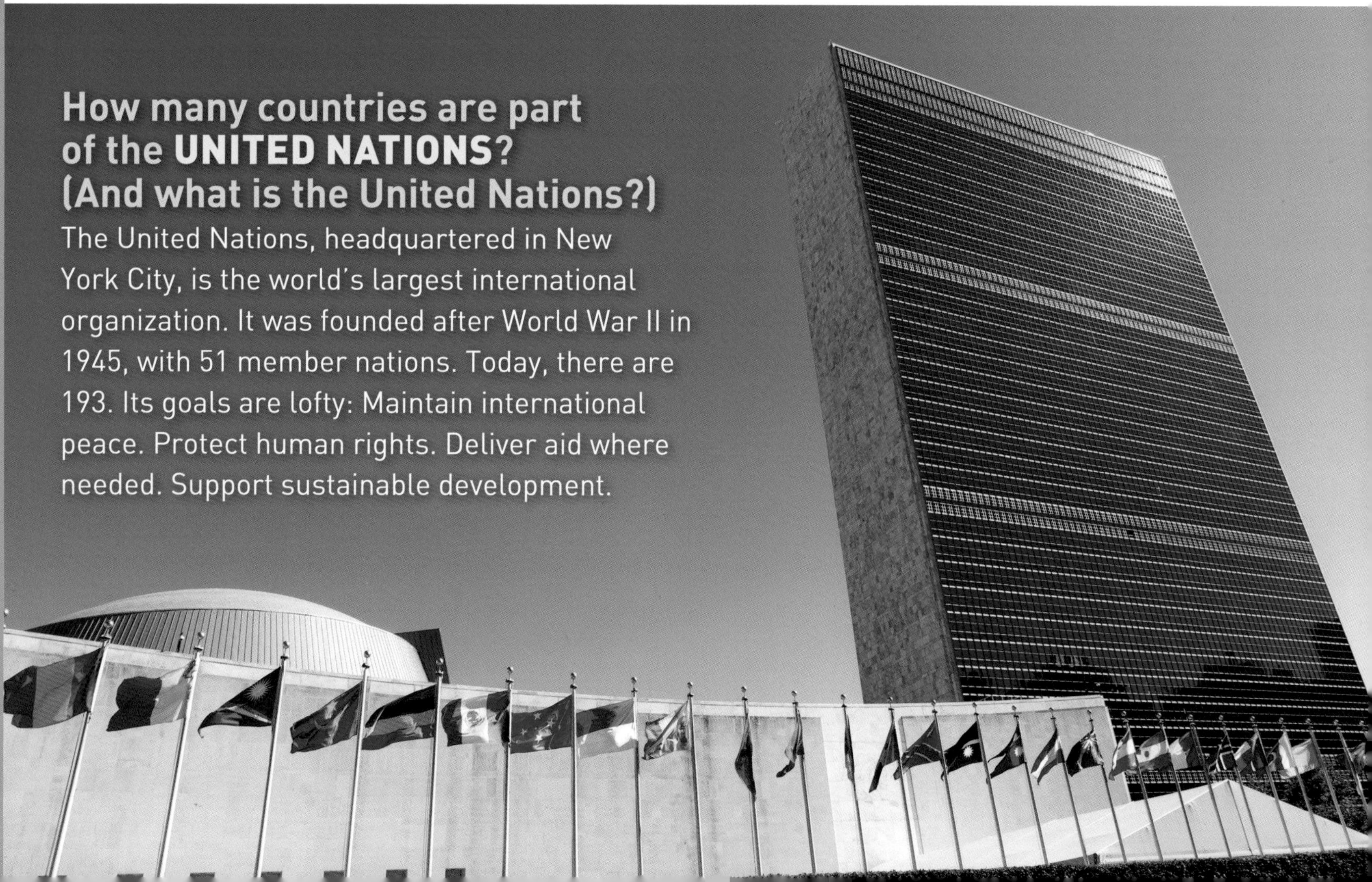

How many countries are part of the **UNITED NATIONS?** (And what is the United Nations?)

The United Nations, headquartered in New York City, is the world's largest international organization. It was founded after World War II in 1945, with 51 member nations. Today, there are 193. Its goals are lofty: Maintain international peace. Protect human rights. Deliver aid where needed. Support sustainable development.

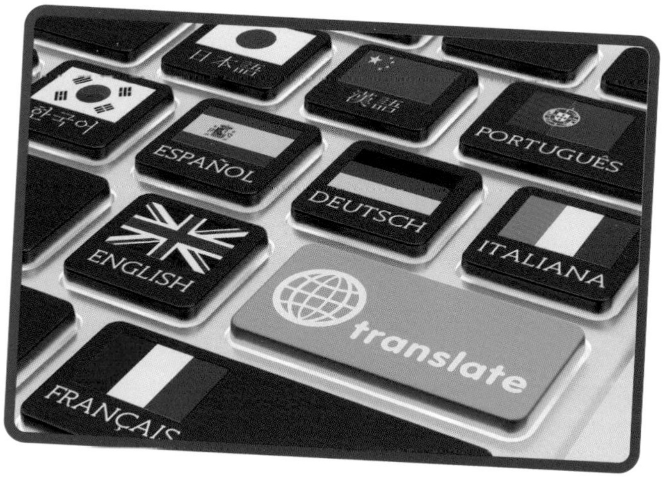

How many **LANGUAGES** do people speak around the globe?

There are more than 7,000 spoken languages in the world. The largest number of spoken languages in a single country is 840, in Papua New Guinea, the island nation just north of Australia. Then comes Indonesia (712), Nigeria (522), and India (454). In fifth place is the United States (326).

How Many People Live in the World's **MOST POPULATED COUNTRIES?***

NATION	POPULATION
China	1,397,897,720
India	1,339,330,514
United States	334,998,398
Indonesia	275,122,131
Pakistan	238,181,034

**The World Factbook*, Central Intelligence Agency (CIA), 2021

Learn More

Go to the Central Intelligence Agency's *World Factbook* for maps, flags, numbers, and other facts for every country, from Afghanistan to Zimbabwe.

- www.cia.gov/the-world-factbook/countries

How many residents live in the world's **SMALLEST COUNTRY?**

The world's least populated nation is Vatican City—home of the pope, the head of the Roman Catholic Church. Also known as the Holy See, Vatican City has about 1,000 residents. Its land is pretty small too. Vatican City covers just 0.17 square miles (0.44 sq km). The National Mall in Washington, D.C., is bigger than that!

IN PLAIN LANGUAGE

Are there any GLOBAL WORDS?

A group of scientists called linguists once recorded informal conversation in more than 30 languages from five continents. All the recordings had one word in common. That word signals a problem, a lack of knowledge related to that problem, and a request for a reply. What is that word? *Huh*. Yup, confusion was the world's most easily shared and understood emotion. Others have suggested a few other globally understood words: *Coke*, *banana*, and *taxi*.

Is SIGN LANGUAGE universal?

No. There are more than 300 different sign languages used by more than 70 million Deaf and hearing-impaired people worldwide. Sign languages have their own rules and grammar. They can be as different as spoken languages from each other. American Sign Language (ASL) is the main language of many North Americans.

Which Languages Have the MOST NATIVE SPEAKERS?*

China, with a population of more than 1.3 billion, tops the list. The world's most commonly spoken language, including native and nonnative speakers, is English.

LANGUAGE	NUMBER OF NATIVE SPEAKERS
Mandarin Chinese	1.1 billion
Spanish	471 million
English	370 million
Hindi	342 million
Arabic	315 million
Portuguese	232 million
Bengali	229 million
Russian	154 million
Japanese	126 million
Lahnda (Western Punjabi)	118 million

*Babbel, 2021

What is the **HARDEST LANGUAGE** to learn if English is your first language? And the easiest?

If your first language is English, you'll need 2,200 hours to pick up Mandarin Chinese, according to the Foreign Service Institute of the U.S. Department of State. Japanese and Korean aren't easy either. Learners must memorize unfamiliar characters. On the easier end, consider Norwegian (Norway), Dutch (Netherlands), Spanish (various countries), and Afrikaans (South Africa). Some of the pronunciations, word order, grammar, and vocabulary are close to English. These languages take an estimated 600 hours to learn. Bon chance!

Why are some **LANGUAGES** considered **ENDANGERED?**

Just like animals, a language can be endangered. If only a few native speakers remain and they are not teaching it to their children, it may disappear. A language may die, or become dormant, when its native speakers take up other languages and use their native language less frequently. Or a language can be forcibly taken. As recently as the 1960s, government schools in the United States and Canada punished Indigenous students for speaking their languages. Today, nearly half of the world's languages are endangered.

Q&A: A Remarkable Person

Luci Tapahonso

Poet and Professor

When and where was she born? 1953, in Shiprock, New Mexico

What is her first language? Diné, the Navajo language

Where was she educated? At a mission boarding school, where she was forbidden to speak her native language, then at Shiprock High School and the University of New Mexico

What has she accomplished? Incorporated her language, traditions, and perspectives into her poetry and teaching

What is the highest honor she has received? Served as the Navajo Nation's first poet laureate (2013–2015)

What did she say? "I consider Navajo language to be the undercurrent, the matrix which everything in my life filters through . . . Yet I use English to function in American society."

NAMES AND PLACES

Why do COUNTRIES change their NAMES?

Name changes are not as infrequent as you'd think. They happen for political reasons, for national pride, and even for marketing or attracting tourists. It's true: the Czech Republic changed its short-form name to the catchy Czechia in 2016, hoping to get more visitors. Swaziland became the Kingdom of eSwatini in 2018, in part to keep it from being confused with Switzerland. Other times, a new nation just needs a name, even an old one. That was the case after the collapse of the Soviet Union in 1991 and Yugoslavia in 1992. Armenia, Estonia, Latvia, Ukraine, and Russia—and 10 others—replaced the name *Soviet Union*. And now it's Bosnia and Herzegovina, Croatia, Kosovo, North Macedonia, Montenegro, Serbia, and Slovenia instead of *Yugoslavia*.

Is it the UNITED KINGDOM, GREAT BRITAIN, or ENGLAND?

People often use any one of these names to refer to the country off the northwestern coast of Europe. But that's not quite right. England, along with Scotland and Wales, is part of Great Britain. Great Britain, along with Northern Ireland, is part of the United Kingdom. The country's official name, the United Kingdom of Great Britain and Northern Ireland, often gets shortened to the UK. Fun fact: In years 500 to 1500, known as the Middle Ages, the name *Britain* also covered a small part of France now known as Brittany. That's why people started to call the big island nearby *Great* Britain.

How are WARS named?

A war can be named after the location of the fighting, like the Vietnam War (1954–1973). It can be named after the two sides fighting, like the Iran-Iraq War (1980–1988). Or after its duration, more or less—the Hundred Years' War (1337–1453). That one was fought between France and England over the French crown. The name can come from the year it began—War of 1812 (it ended in 1815). The way world wars are named makes sense, though the first one was the Great War and only later become World War I (1914–1918).

Q&A: A Remarkable Person

Maya Lin

Sculptor and Architect

When and where was she born? 1959, in Athens, Ohio

What were her childhood pastimes? Board games, playing outside, writing poems, and making art out of clay

What has she accomplished? Won a design competition as a college student for the Vietnam War Memorial in Washington, D.C., that honored more than 58,000 service members killed (opened in 1982)

What else has she accomplished? Designed the Civil Rights Memorial at the Southern Poverty Law Center in Montgomery, Alabama (1989)

What did she say? "I wanted to say something about making this memorial personal, human, and focused on the individual experience. I wanted to honestly present that time and reflect upon our relationship to war and to loss."

Does the COLD WAR have anything to do with winter?

No. A cold—or hot—war can happen in any season. A cold war is conflict that doesn't involve military fighting. A hot war is actual warfare. The so-called Cold War lasted from 1945 to 1989. This conflict took place mostly between the Soviet Union (a communist system with a central government) and the United States (a capitalist system with political parties). Each side also had allies in other nations around the world. The Cold War never heated up into a hot war. But it did result in the building of the Berlin Wall in 1961, major buildups of weapons stockpiles, and other global conflicts.

TIME IS MONEY

When did people first use MONEY?

Before credit cards and mobile payment services, humans pulled out their wallets for the first time about 40,000 years ago. Well, not really wallets. More like their flint tools to trade, or barter, for something else. Archaeological records prove it. Mesopotamians first used coins nearly 5,000 years ago. It took another 3,000 years for paper money to show up, in China.

Why don't we buy things with GOLD anymore?

Gold is valuable. You can use it to make coins or jewelry or spark plugs. In the past, it directly funded trade and wars. So why don't we still use gold this way? Having a gold standard means tying your currency to a specific amount of the shiny metal. A government must buy and sell gold at the set price at any time. Without a gold standard, a nation can adjust interest rates or use other financial tools to make its economy more stable. Need more reasons to get off gold? Mining gold is expensive and damages the environment.

What Nations Produce the MOST GOODS AND SERVICES Per Year?*

NATION	TOTAL
United States	$22.7 trillion
China	$16.6 trillion
Japan	$5.4 trillion
Germany	$4.3 trillion
United Kingdom	$3.1 trillion

*International Monetary Fund, 2021

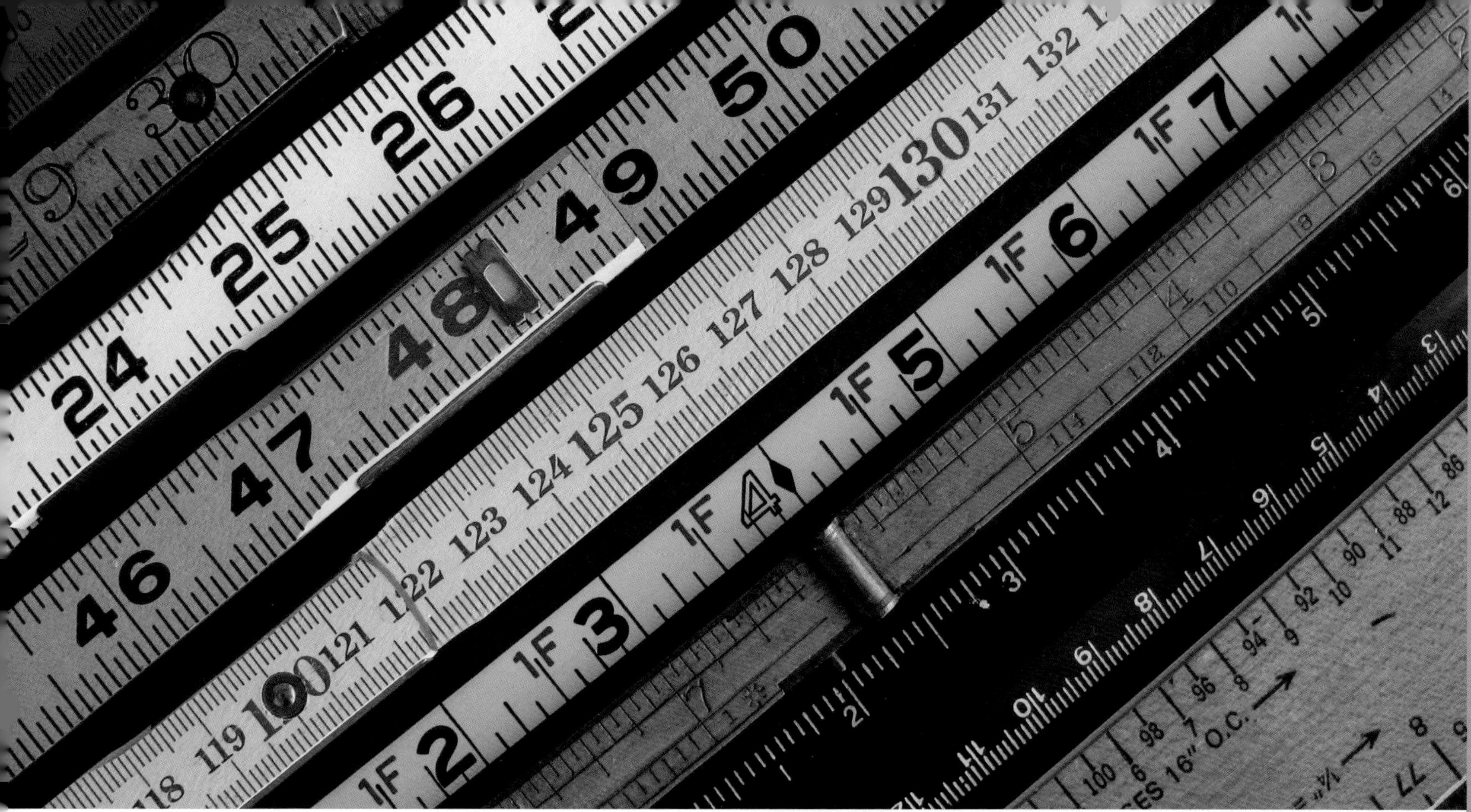

Why doesn't the United States use the METRIC SYSTEM?

Money. Many American industries (and citizens, truth be told) are opposed to making the costly switch. So gas stations deliver fuel in gallons not liters. Road signs continue to feature miles not kilometers. And people expect temperature forecasts in Fahrenheit not Celsius. A big economic advantage of going metric is more straightforward access to various international markets. Many areas of life in the United States—science, medicine, government, maybe even your classroom—are mostly metric. Only two other countries still rely on the British Imperial System of measurement: Liberia and Burma.

Q&A: A Remarkable Person

Esther Duflo

Economist

When and where was she born? 1972, in Paris, France

What was her first interest in school? History, then she decided that economics could be more effective in solving real-world problems

What has she accomplished? Used experiments called randomized control trials to study concrete ways to reduce global poverty; her findings affected policy in dozens of countries

What is the highest honor she has received? Nobel Prize in economics (2019), shared with Abhijit Banerjee and Michael Kremer

What did she say? "What the data is going to be able to do—if there's enough of it—is uncover, in the mess and the noise of the world, some lines of music that actually have harmony. It's there, somewhere."

LEADING THE WAY

What do all HUMAN BEINGS have in common?

No matter what nation, we all have rights as human beings. "All human beings are born free and equal in dignity and rights." This comes from the Universal Declaration of Human Rights. The United Nations adopted the six pages of text in 1948. The declaration set out human rights for all to be protected, agreed on by countries for the first time. Today, you can read that declaration in more than 500 languages, from Abkhaz (spoken in the country of Georgia) to Zulu. It's the most translated document in the world.

Learn More

Go to Amnesty International to see the 30 freedoms laid out in the Universal Declaration of Human Rights.

- www.amnesty.org/en/what-we-do/universal-declaration-of-human-rights

Why do some nations have ROYAL FAMILIES?

It's mostly a question of what parts of its history and heritage a country chooses to embrace or honor. The world has 26 monarchies, with kings, queens, sultans, emperors, and emirs. Monarchs reign or rule, with real political power to different degrees, over 43 countries. A monarch is often symbolic (UK, Sweden, Cambodia). But there are some monarchs who rule (Saudi Arabia, Brunei). And others who have some political powers (Monaco, Thailand).

Why did Egyptian rulers build PYRAMIDS?

Egyptian rulers, or pharaohs, wanted lasting, grand burial places for themselves. And so they ordered structures built—the bigger, the better. About 4,500 years ago in northern Egypt, tens of thousands of workers cut, lugged, and assembled more than 2 million stones, each weighing 2.5 tons (2.3 mt). The Great Pyramid in Giza, which spans 13 acres (5.3 ha), took 20 years to complete.

Q&A: A Remarkable Person

Nelson Mandela

President of South Africa

When and where was he born? 1918, in Transkei, South Africa (he died in 2013)

What was his birth name? Rolihlahla, "pulling a tree branch" or "troublemaker" in Xhosa, the language of his Tembu people (a teacher gave him the name Nelson)

What did he accomplish? Led a movement to end South Africa's system of racial segregation (apartheid), survived 27 years of imprisonment, and then served as president (1994–1999)

What was the highest honor he received? Nobel Peace Prize (1993), along with Frederik Willem de Klerk (then South Africa's president) for "the peaceful termination of the apartheid regime, and for laying the foundations for a new democratic South Africa"

What did he say? "It is not our diversity which divides us; it is not our ethnicity, or religion or culture that divides us. Since we have achieved our freedom, there can only be one division amongst us: between those who cherish democracy and those who do not."

What's the difference between a PRESIDENT and a PRIME MINISTER?

A prime minister runs the government in nations with parliaments (Canada, Japan). Sometimes the person in that role is called a chancellor (Germany). A president heads the government in nations with a presidential system (United States, Brazil, Botswana). Some other nations have a prime minister and a president (France, Russia).

ON THE JOB

Everyone works to make the world run. Most everything that needs doing is done by people. There are all kinds of careers. There are heroes of sports and medicine. There's hard work. Easier work. Well-paid work. Not-as-well-paid work. Dangerous work. Social media work. Nine-to-five work. Jobs that are out, jobs that will be in. Why do pro basketball players earn such huge paychecks? Why are smokejumpers good at sewing? Where did the 40-hour work week come from? It's time to get the job done. Shall we put our noses to the grindstone?

SHOW ME THE MONEY

Why do pro basketball players earn such huge PAYCHECKS?

We love, love, love to watch them play. Millions of people watch the games, especially the big ones—and all those commercials. That's why the TV networks are willing to pay the National Basketball Association and its teams billions of dollars for the right to air them. Then there are ticket sales and team merchandise. NBA sponsorships alone add up to almost $1.5 billion a season. That helps make basketball the world's highest paid sport.

Which Pro Athletes Score the MOST MONEY?*

Professional athletes can make more in a single year than a worker in nearly any other field. Total earnings include prize money, pay, sponsorships, licensing, and appearances.

MEN	EARNINGS
Roger Federer (tennis)	$106.3 million
Cristiano Ronaldo (soccer)	$105.0 million
Lionel Messi (soccer)	$104.0 million
Neymar (soccer)	$95.5 million
LeBron James (basketball)	$88.2 million

WOMEN	EARNINGS
Naomi Osaka (tennis)	$37.4 million
Serena Williams (tennis)	$36.0 million
Ashleigh Barty (tennis)	$13.1 million
Simona Halep (tennis)	$10.9 million
Bianca Andreescu (tennis)	$8.9 million

*Insider, 2020

What does it take to be a successful FORMULA ONE DRIVER?

Traveling 112 miles (180 km) per hour in a broiling cockpit. Heart racing at 180 beats a minute. Sweating off 5 percent of their body weight. Let's say Formula One drivers are in the hot seat during their nearly two-hour races. They experience strong g-forces, up to five times gravity, pushing down especially on their neck and legs. And that's before you get into the possibility of crashing. This is a dangerous sport. It requires years of training, a high level of fitness, and millions of fans. That's you, Lewis Hamilton!

Q&A: A Remarkable Person

Alex Honnold

Professional Rock Climber

When and where was he born? 1985, in Sacramento, California

Why did he start "free solo" climbing as a teenager? His shyness kept him from climbing—and belaying—with others.

What has he accomplished? Became the first person to climb El Capitan in Yosemite National Park, California, without any ropes (2017), captured in the Oscar-winning documentary *Free Solo*

What else has he accomplished? Started the Honnold Foundation to promote solar energy projects around the world

What has he said? "I lived in a van for 10 years. I had a purpose—to be the best climber I could be—so I didn't need many material possessions, and I was probably happier than most people, because I was doing exactly what I loved at the highest level."

Can AMATEUR ATHLETES make money?

Yes. As of 2021, amateur student athletes, like those who play for college teams, may earn money from their names, images, and likenesses (NIL). That means national ad campaigns, paid appearances, and sponsored posts on their social media accounts. The biggest winners are NCAA basketball and football players.

How do professional CLIMBERS earn a living?

The largest paycheck often comes from sponsorships. Outdoor brands like North Face pay climbers to use their products and promote them on social media. For those with an inspirational life story, speaking at corporate events can command considerable fees. Not every sport has a professional league, tour, or circuit. It takes creativity to earn a living in lesser-known sports.

GET A DOCTOR, STAT!

Why are jobs in HEALTH CARE growing?

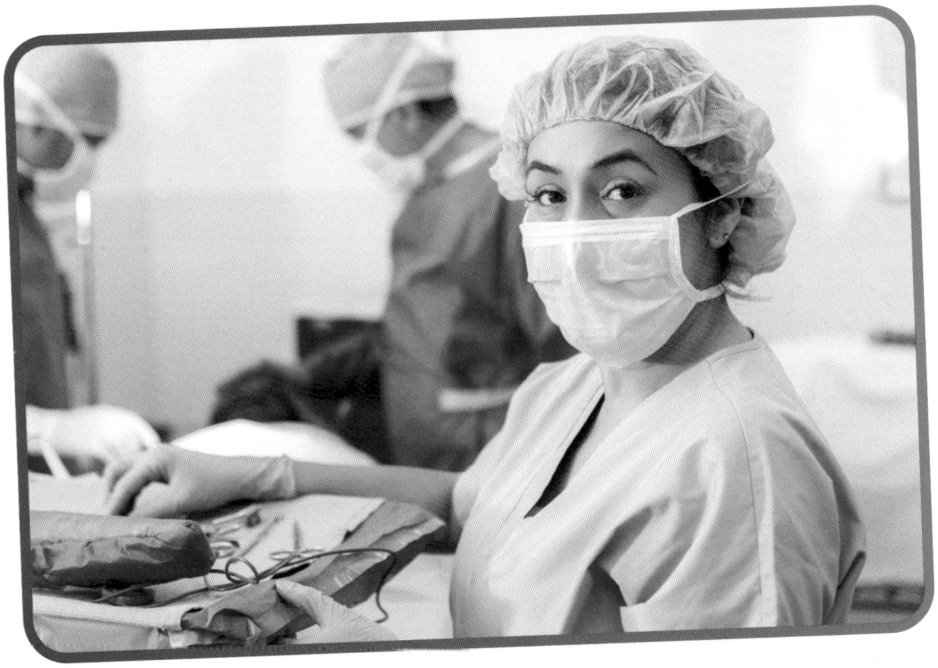

Projections say jobs in health care will grow 16 percent—about 2.6 million new jobs—by 2030. That's mostly due to an aging population, since older people often need more medical care. The fastest-growing demand is for specialty nurses, like midwives and surgical nurses. Those jobs will grow way faster than average (45 percent).

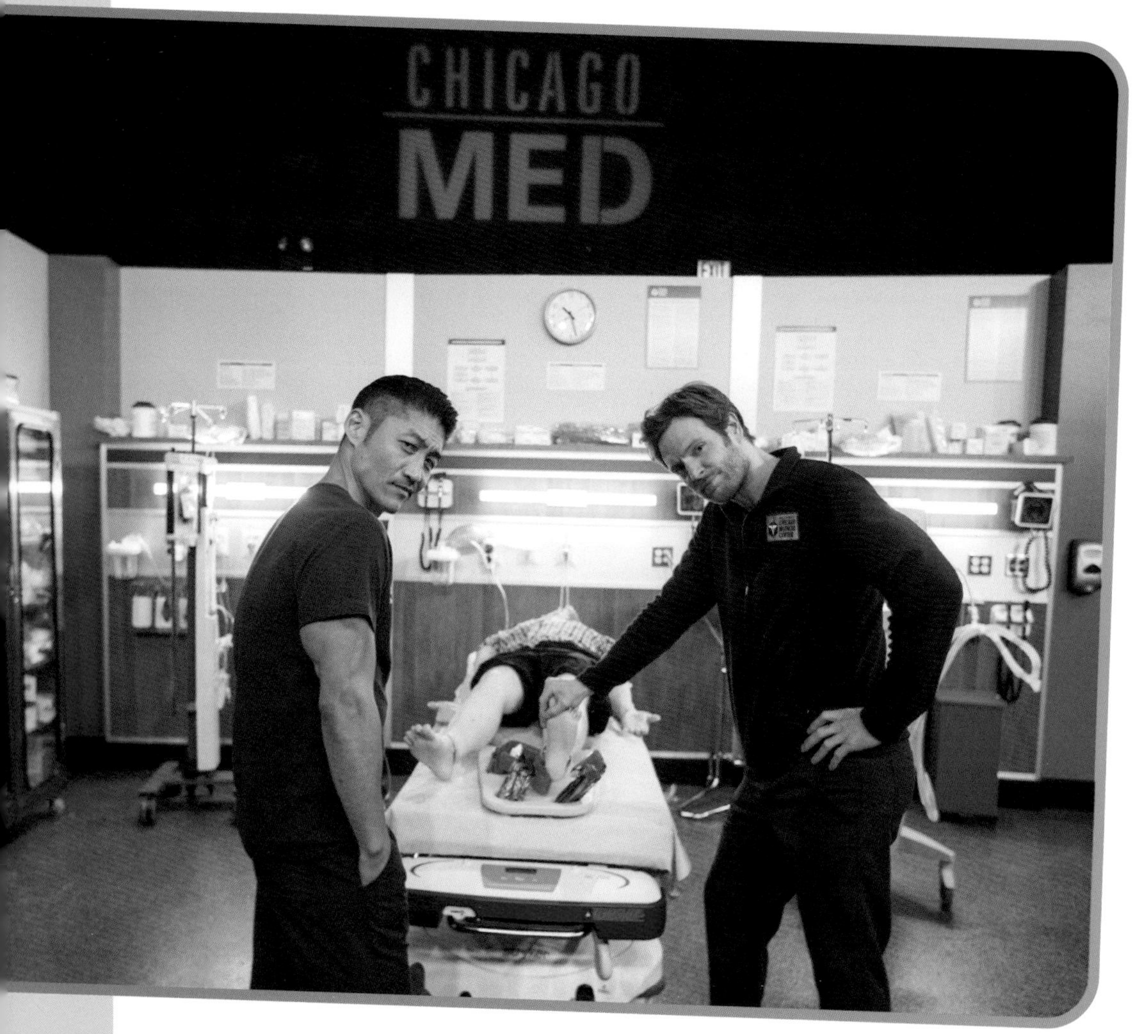

Do TV DRAMAS show what it's really like to work in a hospital?

Your favorite show set in an ER has truth-based storylines, along with plenty of inaccuracies. Doctors are highly specialized. They don't participate in every diagnosis. Dramatic lifesaving techniques like CPR aren't that commonplace. In an actual ER, nurses, radiologists, and lab technicians play much larger roles—and everyone is much too busy for all that socializing! What does seem to be accurate is the TV hospital teams' dedication to patient care.

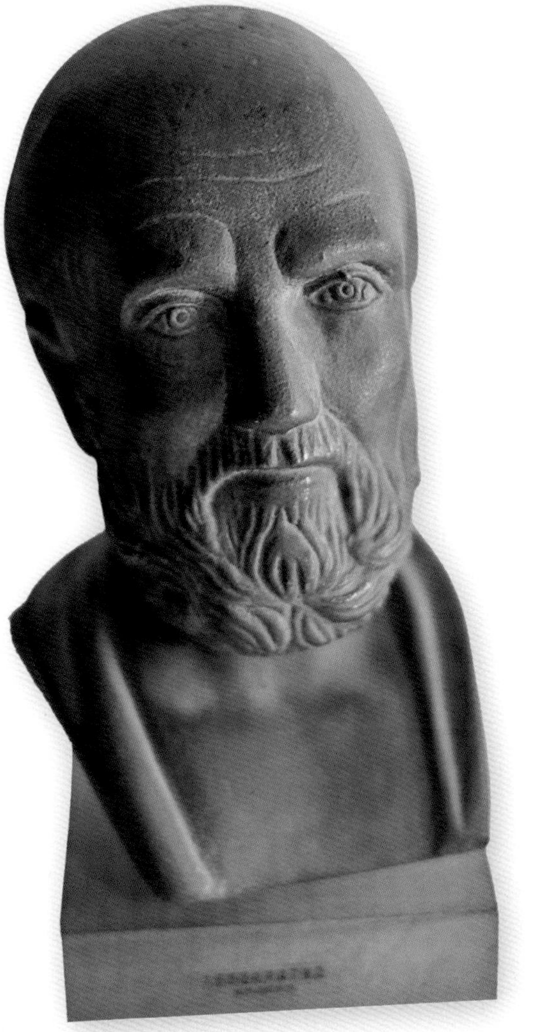

Do doctors still take the HIPPOCRATIC OATH?

The Hippocratic oath continues to be part of nearly all U.S. medical school graduations. In it, new doctors vow to treat the ill to the best of their abilities and to live in an exemplary way. New versions of the oath include a pledge to "advocate for a more equitable health care system from the local to the global level." Hippocrates, a physician from ancient Greece, is often called the father of medicine. His name is part of this ethical code.

Q&A: A Remarkable Person

Jennifer Doudna

Biochemist

When and where was she born? 1964, in Washington, D.C.

When did she realize she wanted to be a scientist? When she was in 11th grade, after a scientist gave a presentation to her school about cancer research, Doudna thought, "I want to be her."

What has she accomplished? Developed a method for genome editing (CRISPR) that can lead to new scientific discoveries and ways to fight cancer and other diseases

What is the highest honor she has received? Nobel Prize in chemistry (2020), along with Emmanuelle Charpentier

What has she said? "In my experience, kids are natural scientists. They're curious about their world and, unless somebody squelches that, they're interested in the world that we inhabit. Why do we look the way we do? Why does our world work the way it does? All those types of questions. Finding ways to encourage that natural curiosity is so important."

Learn More

Go to the Association of American Medical Colleges to find more than 135 specialties for doctors.

- www.aamc.org/cim

WEAR IN THE (WORKING) WORLD?

Why are **SMOKEJUMPERS** good at sewing?

Smokejumpers are wildland firefighters who often travel to work by plane or helicopter. They are trained to parachute into remote areas. Only about 450 jumpers work at nine bases across the western United States. Since there are so few of them, they often have to create their own equipment. That means sewing their jumpsuits, harnesses, and gear bags from scratch. They repair torn parachutes too. Smokejumping bases are even equipped with rigging tables and sewing machines. And sew on.

When did U.S. soldiers start wearing **CAMOUFLAGE**?

U.S. troops wore a kind of camouflage at the end of World War I. (The French first used modern camouflage on cannons in 1915. The French word *camoufler* means "to disguise.") U.S. snipers hid in green burlap suits, covered with tufts of grass, in 1918. Then, U.S. Marines fighting in the Pacific in 1943 wore reversible uniforms—tan "frogs" for the beach and green for the jungle. The next year, some units wore camo invading Normandy in German-occupied France. Fast-forward to 2005, and a pixelated "digicam" camo, with an unusual, video-game look. Today's standard-issue uniform is traditional green and brown camo. Members of the U.S. Army, Air Force, and Space Force wear it.

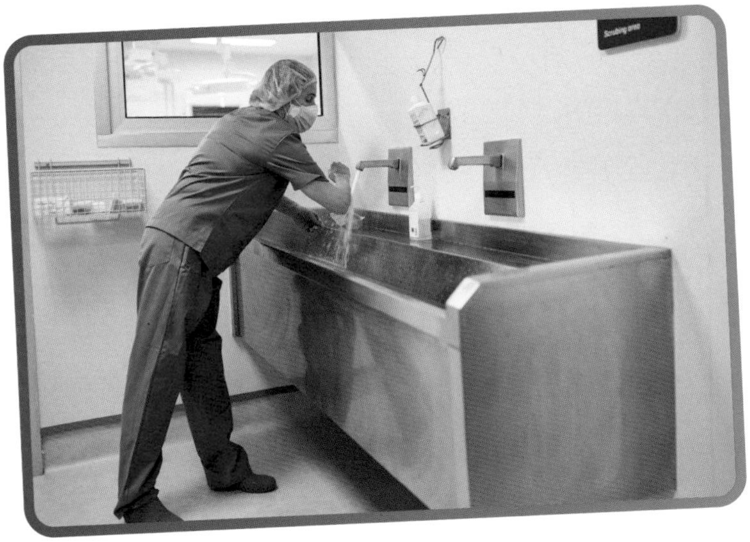

Why are they called **SCRUBS**?

Scrubs are the loose-fitting clothes worn by hospital staff. "Scrubbing in" is what surgical teams do before entering the operating room. They scrub their hands, fingernails, and forearms, then put on sterile gloves and gowns. Originally, nurses and doctors only wore scrubs during surgery. Now, many wear this practical, comfortable clothing all the time.

THE WHYS BEHIND SOME WORK WEAR

Workers often wear uniforms to do their jobs. Here are the whys behind some of their attire.

Airline Pilot

What? Cap
When? Early 1930s
Why? Commercial airline pilots wear a captain's cap with a visor to help identify them to others. Wearing it also conveys a professionalism that can reassure nervous airline passengers. But not every airline requires a cap as part of its official pilot uniform.

Chef

What? Tall white hat
When? 1800s
Why? A traditional chef's uniform includes a white toque (from the Arabic *taq* for "round"). Toques are white to signal the kitchen's cleanliness. The most senior chef usually wears the tallest hat. Today, skull caps, head wraps, and baseball hats are other ways of addressing the more practical reason to wear a hat in the kitchen: keeping hair from falling into food.

Doctor

What? White lab coat
When? Late 19th century
Why? At first, the white lab coat distinguished a trained medical professional from traveling quacks. The garment conveyed scientific rigor and helped identify doctors in busy clinics. In practice, doctor's coats can carry dangerous bacteria and transmit infection. Fresh scrubs are more hygienic and appear friendlier to patients. In fact, some physicians don't wear the garment to prevent "white coat syndrome." That's an unusually high blood pressure recording, due entirely to anxiety from seeing a doctor in an imposing white coat.

OCCUPIED, PAST AND PRESENT

What Are Some Jobs of THE PAST?*

Occupations come and go with society's needs and technological developments. Here are the whys behind some professions no longer in the job listings.

Ice Cutter

When? 19th century until the 1930s
What did they do? Cut up ice on frozen lakes for cold food storage in cellars and ice boxes
What now? Electric refrigerators and freezers

Knocker-upper

When? 19th century until the 1970s, in some areas of the UK
What did they do? Knocked on factory workers' windows and doors with long sticks to wake them up before their shift
What now? Alarm clocks, including cellphone alarms

Lamplighter

When? 19th century and early 20th century
What did they do? Used long poles to light, extinguish, and refuel gas street lamps
What now? Timed electric- or solar-powered streetlights

Lector

When? Early 1900s
What did they do? Read newspapers and books aloud to entertain factory workers during their shifts
What now? Radio, streaming music apps, audio books, and podcasts

Soda Jerk

When? 1920s through the 1950s
What did they do? Served soda, sundaes, and ice cream from a counter, often in a drugstore, called a soda fountain
What now? Drive-through fast-food restaurants

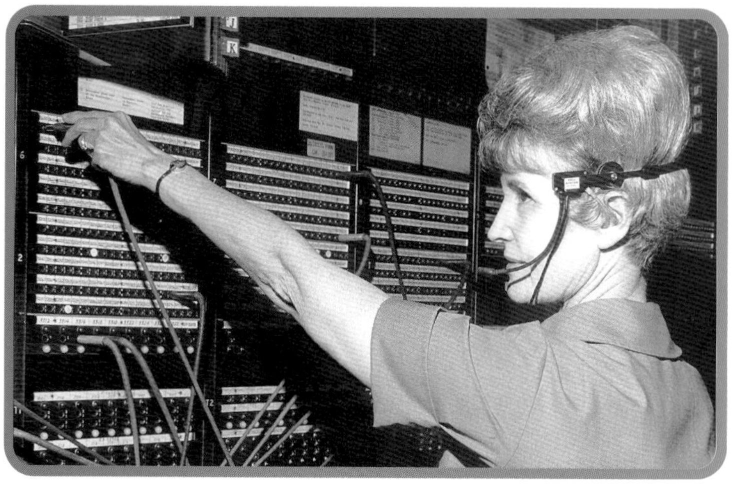

Switchboard Operator

When? 19th century and early 20th century
What did they do? Connected telephone calls between two people using manual plugs and switches
What now? Cellphones

*Stacker, 2020

What Are Some Jobs of THE FUTURE?*

It's hard work to imagine the occupations of tomorrow. Some estimates say that by 2030, automation could replace as many as one-quarter of the U.S. workforce. But there will be plenty of demand for new professions also. Here are the whys behind some possible top jobs in 2030.

Artificial Intelligence (AI) Specialist

What will they do? Help companies use technology, robots, and tools to automate and streamline daily operations

How to prepare? Major in computer science, information technology, or engineering

Digital Currency Adviser

What will they do? Provide financial planning for customers' digital wealth, from online accounts to virtual gaming assets

How to prepare? Study accounting and data security

Rewilder

What will they do? Restore environmentally damaged areas by reintroducing nature

How to prepare? Study environmental science, agriculture, and city planning

Smart Home Designer

What will they do? Work with homeowners and work-from-home employees to set up computer-operated, or "smart," climate control, lighting, audio, and security systems

How to prepare? Study interior design and keep up with latest technological advances

Space Pilot

What will they do? Guide commercial spacecraft at speeds exceeding 2,000 miles (3,200 km) per hour

How to prepare? Study astronautics and train as an airline pilot

*Resumeble, 2021

ONLINE OCCUPATIONS

What do SOCIAL MEDIA INFLUENCERS do?

Social media influencers use their platform to generate interest in something, usually something one can buy. They are known for their expertise on such topics as beauty products, cooking, guitar playing, or magic. Influencers have the trust of their followers and keep them engaged with regular posts. They can have millions of followers (that's you, Kylie Jenner!) or a small, specialized following (calling all owners of cute pets!).

Can social media INFLUENCING be a CAREER?

Yes, it could be. There are a few possible streams of income. Companies pay influencers for posts about their products—that's called sponsored content—and hire them as brand ambassadors. Influencers may earn a percentage of sales generated from links in their posts. Those who blog sell advertising on their websites. Many also sell their own products, including courses, subscriptions, and ebooks. That can add up to real money. It's a lot of work, and some luck is required to succeed.

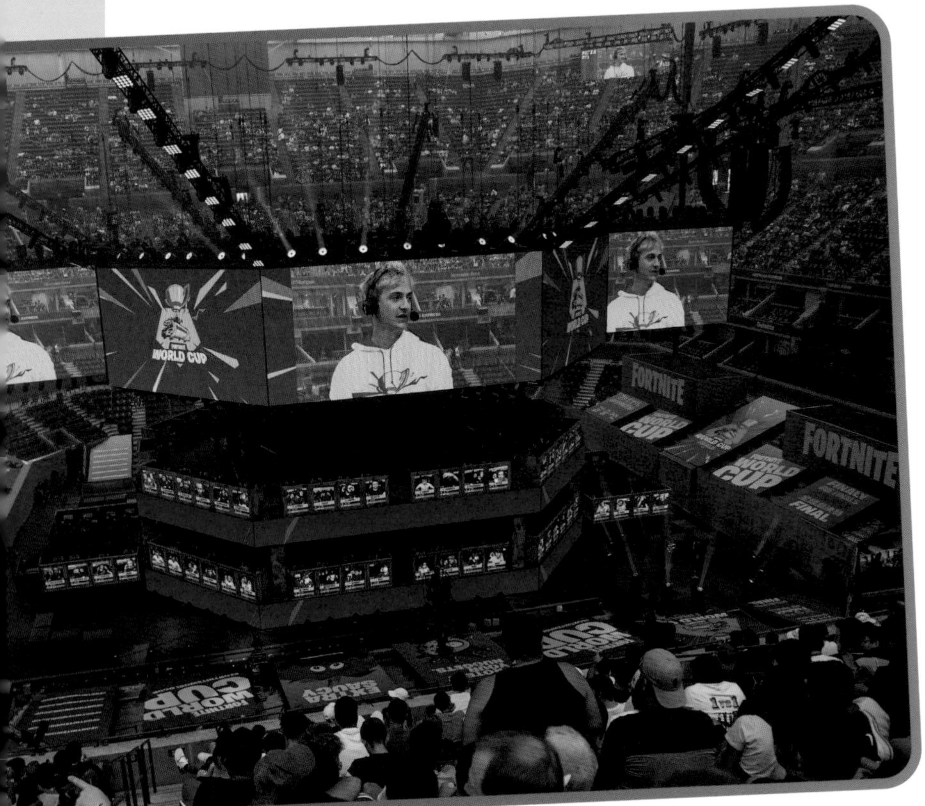

Could you ever earn a paycheck playing VIDEO GAMES?

It's possible but not easy. The best-paid gamers make money livestreaming their gameplay on Twitch or YouTube. They win gaming tournaments and earn sponsorships or even salaries from e-sports teams. But there are other ways to earn money in this field. You could write reviews or news articles for a gaming website. You could create and sell video game guides or write an ebook. You could host a regular gaming podcast or a YouTube channel. You could test games for pay. But it might turn your fun into drudgery. If you enjoy playing games, you might want to keep it that way.

Why do YOUTUBERS earn so much money?
"Like, share, comment on this video. Subscribe to my YouTube channel. And don't forget to click on that bell icon to get regular updates!" This call for action increases watch time and engagement. Based on those numbers, YouTube, in turn, suggests the video to others, which increases interest in that channel. YouTubers make money from each ad view. The most successful among them earn even more from merchandise, promoting products, and sponsorships. All YouTube channels start with one—often funny, personal—video.

Who Are the World's TOP SOCIAL MEDIA INFLUENCERS?*

INFLUENCER	FOLLOWERS (Twitter, YouTube, Facebook, and Instagram)	PAYOUTS PER POST ON INSTAGRAM
Cristiano Ronaldo	517 million	$1,604,000
Justin Bieber	455 million	$1,112,000
Ariana Grande	429 million	$1,510,000
Selena Gomez	425 million	$1,468,000
Taylor Swift	361 million	$1,012,000

*Visual Capitalist, 2021; Hopper HQ, 2021

Make a Difference

Find a worthy cause. Work with your family to create an entertaining video to promote it. Ask an organization to post it on its social media.

DANGER, DANGER

Why don't ACTORS perform their own STUNTS?

Flying through the air on a motorcycle, hanging off a rock wall, fighting with hands and swords, swimming with sharks. It's all dangerous work. That's why trained stunt doubles do the potentially life-threatening action sequences. The show (or movie) must go on, and that's not possible if the lead actor is injured. Using stunt doubles also helps production teams save time and money. A second-unit director can shoot with the stunt double while the actor films on the set with the main director. Some actors—Charlize Theron, Adam Driver, and Tom Cruise—do some of their own stunts, though that must be approved by the film's backers.

Do WIND TURBINE technicians suffer from fear of heights?

Some do, at least at first. They have to climb, weighed down with equipment, hundreds of feet to the top of tower ladders. But most technicians, or wind techs, get over it quickly. To do the job, they have to. Maintaining and repairing turbines, the huge devices that turn wind energy into electricity, is a high growth field. It does not usually require a degree but is well paid. And besides, conquering fear helps make the world more environmentally friendly.

Q&A: A Remarkable Person

Michelle Yeoh

Actor and stunt performer

When and where was she born? 1962, in Ipoh, Perak, Malaysia

When did she start studying ballet? When she was four (she stopped at age 16 after a back injury)

How did she get her start in stunt work? Action films in the 1990s

What has she accomplished? Starred in *Crouching Tiger, Hidden Dragon* (2000), the highest-grossing non-English-language film in U.S. history

What else has she appeared in? *Star Trek: Discovery* (2017–2020), *Crazy Rich Asians* (2018) and *Shang-Chi and the Legend of the Ten Rings* (2021)

What has she said? "I gravitate towards roles where women find strength in very difficult, uncompromising situations but maintain clarity in mind, discipline at heart, and a certain strength in spirit."

Why is working as an ICE ROAD TRUCKER dangerous?

Almost anything can take you down: a crack in the ice, the frigid cold, your broken-down truck, bad weather, or poor visibility. The ice that you drive your 70-ton (64 mt) cargo truck across in Alaska and northern Canada must be at least 40 inches (102 cm) thick. Then you must drive no faster than 15 miles (24 km) per hour to reduce movement of the water under the ice. Two trucks passing can cause waves moving in opposite directions to burst through the ice. You might earn as much as $100,000 a year, but it's lonely out there.

What Are the MOST DANGEROUS JOBS in America?*

JOB	FATAL INJURIES PER 100,000	CAUSES
Fishing and hunting	145	Transportation incidents
Logging	69	Contact with objects and equipment
Aircraft pilots and flight engineers	62	Transportation incidents
Roofers	54	Falls, slips, and trips
Construction	40	Transportation incidents

*U.S. Bureau of Labor and Statistics, 2019

ALL IN A DAY'S WORK

Why do we tip? Do we TIP MORE for bills given with a little candy?

There are five reasons we tip, says a professor at Cornell University's School of Hotel Administration. We tip to show off, help the server, get better service in the future, avoid disapproval, or fulfill a sense of duty. And yes, after-dinner candy with the bill increases a server's tips. During COVID-19, tips grew larger as a way of recognizing the risks that workers took to serve others. Keep up those sweet rewards, many say.

Where did the 40-HOUR work week come from?

In 1914, Henry Ford, founder of the Ford Motor Company, set a six-day, 48-hour work week for his workers. Then, in 1926, believing employees could be more productive in fewer hours, he gave them Saturdays off—and offered a pay raise! It was the birth of the five-day 40-hour work week. A 40-hour work week became law in 1940. A big shift into working from home during COVID-19 has changed the way people schedule their work hours yet again. Now, flexibility is the name of the work game—at least away from the assembly line.

Why are women often PAID LESS than men? Isn't it ILLEGAL?

Yes. Employers must pay the same wages for equal work in jobs requiring the same skill, effort, and responsibility. (Congress passed the Equal Pay Act in 1963.) But in 2020, U.S. women earned 82 percent of what men did. Some professions that pay less, on average—like teaching or nursing—employ more women than men. But discrimination still accounts for some of the difference in pay. When people have children, data shows that wages in any field tend to go up for fathers and down for mothers. People who study the question say that offering paid leave and flexible working hours for all new parents—and others needing to balance family-care needs—is a change that could make a big impact.

Why do we call them WHITE-COLLAR and BLUE-COLLAR workers?

People working in traditional offices were first called white-collar workers, for their collared shirts, in 1910. By the 1920s, the term *blue-collar worker* was coined after the sturdier denim or chambray shirts worn by many manual laborers. Some people call artists no-collar workers. They dress in T-shirts.

What Are the Top 10 BEST JOBS Today?*

This list was created based on specific measures. These U.S. jobs pay well and provide interesting challenges, with room to grow professionally and personally. Required degrees range from bachelor's (4 years in college), master's (1 or 2 years after college), and doctorate (5 to 7 years after college).

JOB	SALARY	DEGREE
Physician assistant (care for patients, with licensed physicians)	$112,260	Master's
Software developer (design computer software and/or mobile apps)	$107,510	Bachelor's
Nurse practitioner (care for patients)	$109,820	Master's
Medical and health services manager (run medical practices, nursing homes, hospitals, and clinics)	$100,980	Bachelor's
Physician (care for patients)	$206,500	Doctorate
Statistician (use mathematical models to collect and interpret data)	$91,160	Master's
Speech-language pathologist (work with people who have difficulty speaking or swallowing)	$79,120	Master's
Data scientist (analyze large sets of data)	$94,280	Bachelor's
Dentist (care for patients' teeth)	$155,600	Doctorate
Veterinarian (care for animals)	$95,460	Doctorate

*U.S. News & World Report, 2021

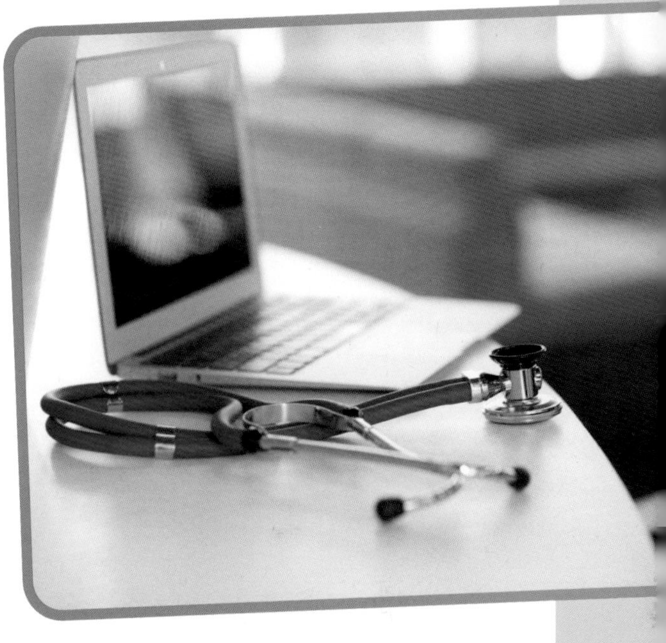

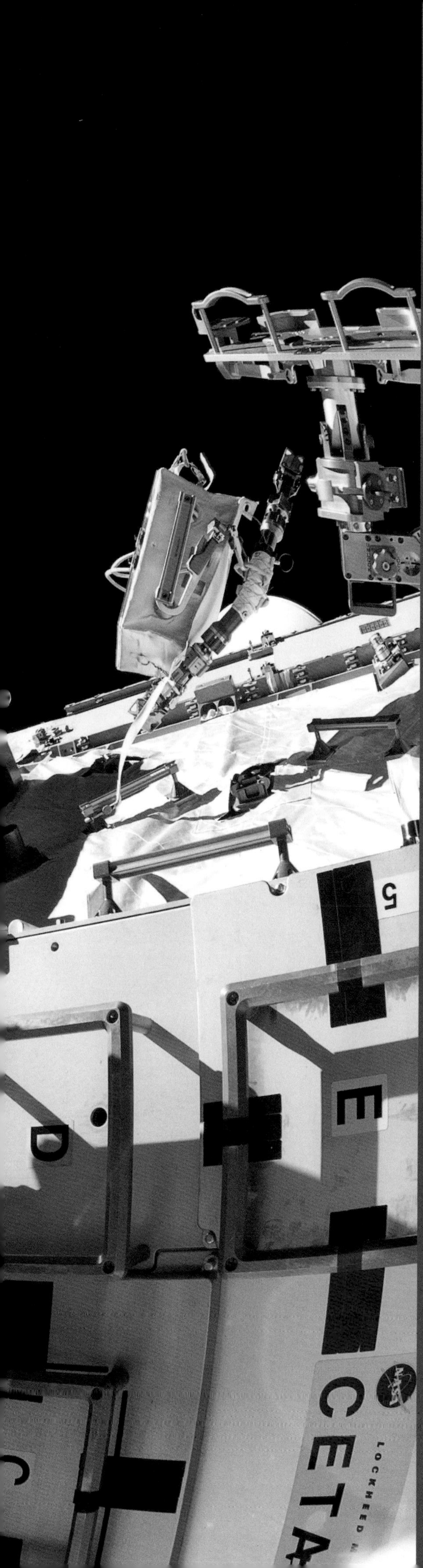

SCIENCE AND SPACE

Pondering what is around us—from the tiniest particle to beyond the universe—raises big questions. Science helps explain many of them. But for those still unanswered, perhaps you'll make scientific discoveries of your own. Discovery starts with curiosity. Is there life on other planets? What happened to the dinosaurs? How do black holes form? What is happiness? The first step is data gathering. Experiment with what follows.

BIG QUESTIONS

What makes the sky **BLUE**?

When the Sun won't come out to play. Ha! Now for the actual answer. The gases and particles in Earth's atmosphere scatter light from the Sun in all directions. Each color has a different wavelength. Blue light scatters more than other colors because it travels as shorter, smaller waves. That's why the sky often looks blue.

How do you explain **INFINITY**?

It is a concept. Infinity is not an actual number. Nothing ever reaches it (if it did, it wouldn't be infinity). Adding one to infinity still equals infinity. It is endless.

Does anything lie **BEYOND OUR UNIVERSE**?

According to the big bang theory, the universe began from a single extremely hot and dense point (called a singularity) nearly 14 billion years ago. In a fraction of a second, that point exploded, creating time, space, and matter. It's not easy to visualize—the expansion of a tiny point into a universe. Not only that, the universe is still expanding at an increasing rate. Is there anything beyond it? Are there alternate universes out there? Are we in a long but endless loop of big bang events? These questions boggle the mind. Theoretical physicists are scientists who try to find answers to these questions—or just a small part of them.

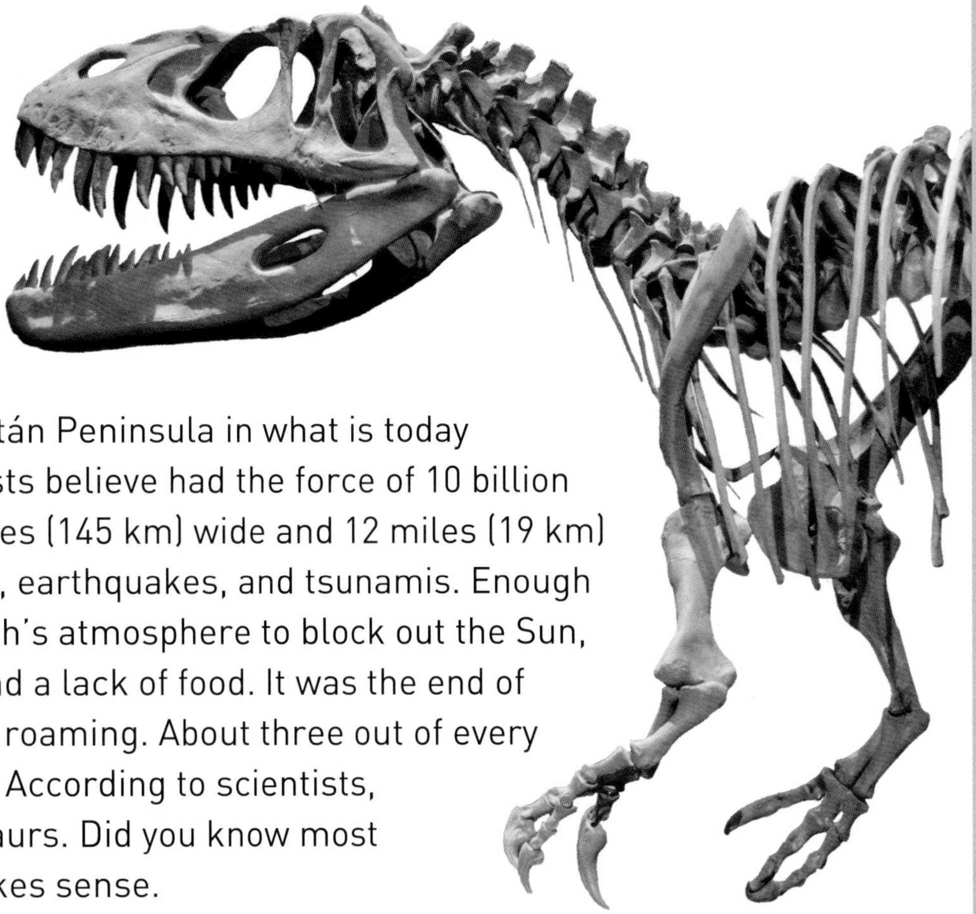

What happened to the **DINOSAURS?**

Well, you probably know dinosaurs big and small used to roam the planet. Then, one day, 66 million years ago, a huge object—most likely an asteroid—hit near the Yucatán Peninsula in what is today Mexico. That asteroid, which scientists believe had the force of 10 billion atomic bombs, created a hole 90 miles (145 km) wide and 12 miles (19 km) deep. The impact triggered wildfires, earthquakes, and tsunamis. Enough ash, dust, and smoke swirled in Earth's atmosphere to block out the Sun, leading to a drop in temperatures and a lack of food. It was the end of dinosaurs, after 165 million years of roaming. About three out of every four animal species were wiped out. According to scientists, today's birds descended from dinosaurs. Did you know most dinosaurs laid eggs? Guess that makes sense.

What is **HAPPINESS?**

It might be a sunny day. Or a snuggle with your pet. Or a win of some kind. But happiness is more than a string of joyful things. Psychologists say part of feeling happy is being able to deal with unhappy feelings along the way, like sadness, anxiety, or boredom. Putting those feelings into words can help. Sounds like a good recipe for happiness.

Which is better: **CAKE or PIE?**

Cake, definitely cake. Unless it's chocolate pie. Then, definitely pie. (Your opinion may vary!)

Make a Difference

Do you ever feel overwhelmed? Try doing something nice—for yourself! Go for a walk. Chat with a family member or friend. Take a nap. Make yourself a little snack.

SMALL QUESTIONS

What is the SMALLEST THING in the world?

A quark. All matter is made from tiny particles called atoms. Protons and neutrons are what make up the core, or nucleus, of an atom, with tiny electrons clouding around it. Protons and neutrons are made up of quarks. Scientists have not been able to split them into anything smaller. Quarks appear to be fundamental particles of matter.

Which ANIMAL is Earth's tiniest?

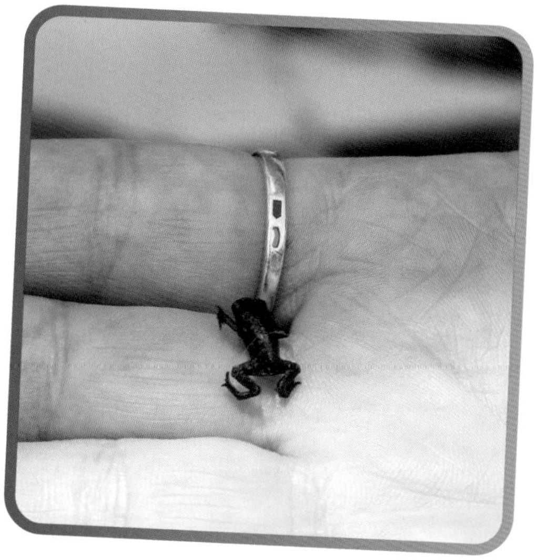

Earth is home to many species of tiny organisms, or living things. But you'd need a microscope to see most of them. The smallest known vertebrate—or animal with a backbone—is called Paedophryne amauensis. Herpetologists, scientists who specialize in reptiles and amphibians, first discovered the tiny frog in 2009. Dark brown with silver spots, it feeds on insects in the tropical forests of Papua New Guinea. The frog measures 0.3 inches (7.7 mm). It can sit on a dime with plenty of room to spare.

Are BLUE MOONS actually rare?

According to the old saying, if something happens "once in a blue moon," it is infrequent. We call a second full moon in a calendar month a "monthly blue moon," though it usually looks pale gray and white—not blue at all. This kind of blue moon occurs every two or three years. A moon that actually appears blue in the night sky is rarer. You can see that kind of blue moon when Earth's atmosphere contains smoke or dust particles from volcanic eruptions or forest fires.

Why is PLUTO a DWARF PLANET?

Pluto, discovered by astronomers in 1930, used to be considered the solar system's smallest planet. Then, in 2006, scientists in the International Astronomical Union agreed on an official definition for the word *planet*. At the same time, they announced Pluto would be defined as a "dwarf planet." Unlike the eight planets in Earth's solar system, Pluto is not big enough to clear other objects around its orbit. Its new classification has been debated around Earth, but science is science.

Is it true that ASTRONAUTS are younger when they return from ORBIT?

Yes. But not by much. For each day astronauts spend in orbit, they will be 0.000023 seconds younger. A year spent on the International Space Station would make one about 0.0085 seconds younger. It's due to something Albert Einstein proved—time dilation, the idea that time passes more slowly as one moves faster. The high orbital speed of the spacecraft means its passengers are moving faster than people on Earth's surface.

Q&A: A Remarkable Person

Albert Einstein

Physicist

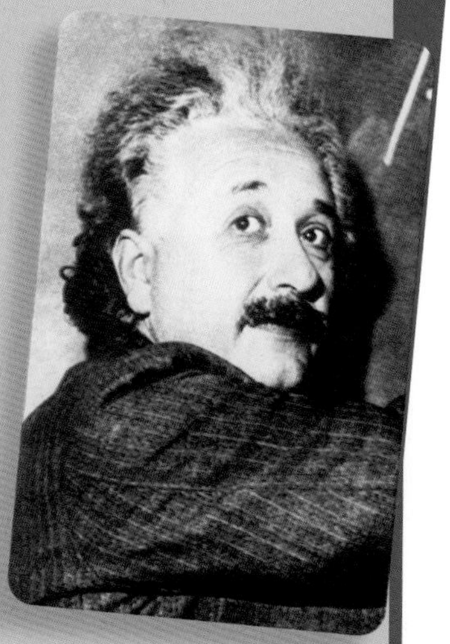

When and where was he born? 1879, in Ulm, Germany (he died in 1955)

What did he start at age six? Playing the violin, which he did with great skill for the rest of his life

What did he accomplish? Developed theories of relativity that further our understanding of time, space, energy, matter, and gravity

What is the highest honor he received? Nobel Prize in physics (1921)

What did he say? "One thing I have learned in a long life: that all our science, measured against reality, is primitive and childlike—and yet it is the most precious thing we have."

DOWN TO A SCIENCE

Who was the **FIRST SCIENTIST?**

The first genuine scientist might have been the ancient Greek thinker Aristotle, who lived in the fourth century BCE. All theories, according to him, must be based on observed facts. He invented the science of reasoning, or logic, and made contributions to the fields of astronomy, biology, physics, and zoology.

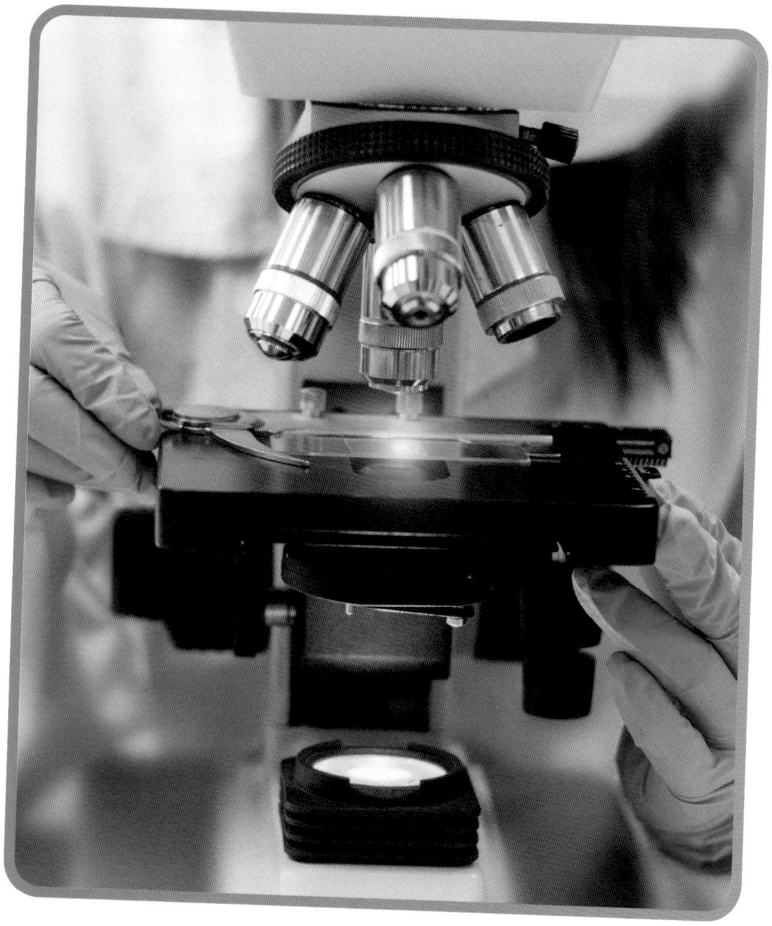

Do all scientists use the SCIENTIFIC METHOD?

Yes. No matter their field, scientists look for answers supported by evidence and logic. Here's a short explanation of their method: Make observation. Ask question. Form hypothesis, or testable explanation, in response to the question. Make prediction. Test prediction. Analyze the data. Accept, reject, or modify hypothesis. Share with others. See if other results match yours. Prepare Nobel Prize speech.

Make a Difference

Use each step of the scientific method to solve a real-life problem. Light bulb not working? A potted plant dying? A lost phone? Noisy pet parakeet? Saving up your allowance? Family members late to meals?

WHAT ARE THE SCIENCES?

Life science deals with the living, or organic, world. The study of the nonliving, or inorganic, world is called physical science. Social science covers human behavior in a society. Some sciences involve more than one discipline. Environmental science integrates geology, biology, chemistry, and social sciences to address environmental issues.

LIFE SCIENCES

FIELD	STUDY OF ...	SOME BRANCHES
Biology	Living things	Botany (plants), genetics (heredity), marine biology (ocean life), zoology (animals)
Medicine	Health	Immunology (immune system), veterinary (animals)

PHYSICAL SCIENCES

FIELD	STUDY OF ...	SOME BRANCHES
Astronomy	All objects outside Earth's atmosphere	Astrophysics (physics of universe), cosmology (origin of universe)
Chemistry	Matter and its chemical changes	Biochemistry (living things)
Geology	Earth's physical features and history	Paleontology (fossils), mineralogy
Mathematics	Numbers and symbols	Calculus, geometry, logic, statistics
Physics	Matter and forces that act on it	Nuclear physics, quantum (small particles) physics

SOCIAL SCIENCES

FIELD	STUDY OF ...	SOME BRANCHES
Economics	Wealth	Macroeconomics (whole economy), microeconomics (individuals)
Psychology	Human mind and emotions	Child psychology, cognitive (problem solving) psychology
Sociology	Social groups	Criminology (crime and law), urban sociology (cities)

IT'S UNIVERSAL

What's Out There?*

Earth orbits the Sun in our solar system. The Sun is a star in the Milky Way Galaxy. And that galaxy is one of billions in the universe. Here is more information about what's out there.

The Solar System

What is it? The Sun and all the objects that orbit it, such as the eight planets, dwarf planets (like Pluto), dozens of moons, and millions of smaller bodies such as asteroids and comets
How big is it? It is about 179 billion miles (288 billion km) across, by one measure. If the Sun were smaller than a grain of sand, the solar system could fit in the palm of your hand.
When did it form? About 4.5 billion years ago

The Milky Way Galaxy

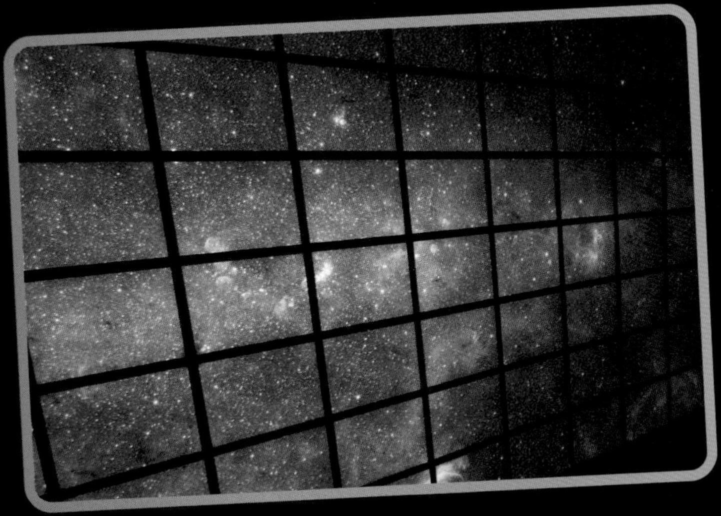

What is it? A large spiral system of 200 to 400 billion stars, including the Sun
How big is it? It is about 100,000 light-years across. (A light-year is the distance light travels in one year.) If the solar system could fit in the palm of your hand, the Milky Way galaxy would span North America.
When did it form? About 13.5 billion years ago

The Universe

What is it? All of the galaxies; everything that exists throughout space and time
How big is it? The visible universe is estimated to be 93 billion light-years across. The rest of the universe, which is not visible, is far larger, though unknown.
When did it form? About 13.8 billion years ago, according to the big bang theory

*National Aeronautics and Space Administration (NASA), 2021

Why don't we FEEL EARTH MOVING?

It's true that Earth moves constantly—on its axis once a day (like a basketball spinning on a finger) and around the Sun once a year. Earth rotates on its axis at about 1,000 miles (1,600 km) per hour. And it journeys around the Sun at about 67,000 miles (108,000 km) per hour. But we don't feel any of this movement because the speeds are constant. Imagine being in a car driving at the same speed on a smooth road. You'd only really feel motion if the car slowed down or sped up.

How many humans have been to the MOON?

24. So far, the Moon is the only celestial body beyond Earth that humans have visited. Americans Neil Armstrong and Buzz Aldrin stepped first on the moon on July 20, 1969, with NASA mission *Apollo 11*.

Why is it called the MILKY WAY galaxy?

The Milky Way galaxy is named after the Milky Way, a hazy band of gas clouds and stars that is visible in Earth's night sky. The ancient Romans called it the *Via Lactea*, or "the road of milk." That is because the Milky Way's appearance is . . . well, milky.

WHAT PLANET ARE YOU ON?

The Whats and Whys Behind the PLANETS IN OUR SOLAR SYSTEM*

There are eight full-sized planets in our solar system. Two are gas giants. They consist mostly of hydrogen and helium. Two are ice giants. They have a small rocky core and a thick icy "soup" of water, ammonia, and methane. The other four are terrestrial, or rocky, planets. Some planets have ring systems of rock, ice, and dust surrounding them. Scientists cannot say for sure what causes planetary rings.

Mercury

How wide is it? 3,032 miles (4,880 km)
What is its average surface temperature? 332°F (167°C)
Where is it in the solar system? Closest to the Sun
What type of planet is it? Terrestrial; no rings
Why is it special? It's the smallest planet.

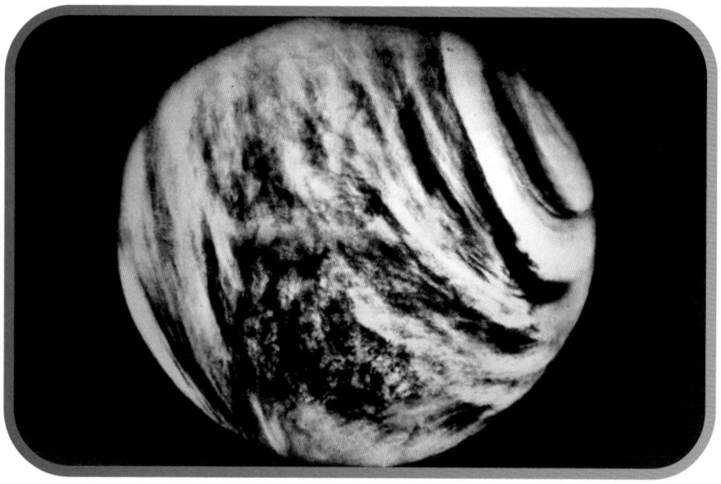

Venus

How wide is it? 7,521 miles (12,104 km)
What is its average surface temperature? 880°F (471°C)
Where is it in the solar system? Second closest to the Sun
What type of planet is it? Terrestrial; no rings
Why is it special? It's the hottest planet.

Earth

How wide is it? 7,918 miles (12,742 km)
What is its average surface temperature? 61°F (16°C)
Where is it in the solar system? Third closest to the Sun
What type of planet is it? Terrestrial; no rings
Why is it special? It's the only planet with human life and the only planet covered mostly in water (about 70 percent).

Mars

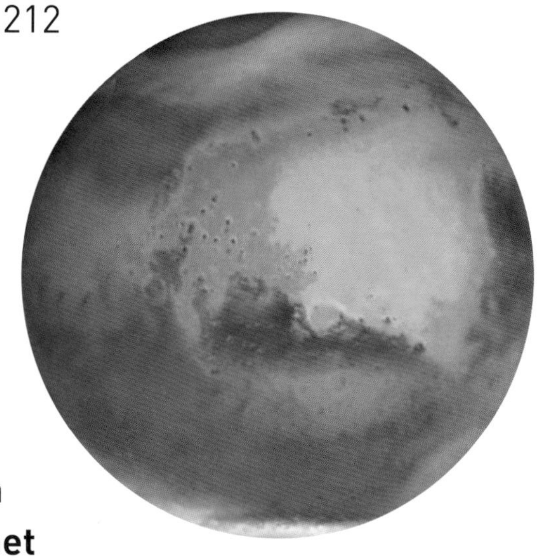

How wide is it? 4,212 miles (6,779 km)
What is its average surface temperature? −20°F (−28°C)
Where is it in the solar system? Fourth closest to the Sun
What type of planet is it? Terrestrial; no rings
Why is it special? It's the only red-appearing planet, due to rusty iron in the ground.

Jupiter

How wide is it? 86,881 miles (139,822 km)
What is its average surface temperature? −162°F (−108°C)
Where is it in the solar system? Fifth closest to the Sun
What type of planet is it? Gas giant; rings
Why is it special? It's the biggest planet.

Saturn

How wide is it? 72,367 miles (116,464 km)
What is its average surface temperature? −218°F (−138°C)
Where is it in the solar system? Sixth closest to the Sun
What type of planet is it? Gas giant; rings
Why is it special? It's the only planet with a large ring system.

Uranus

How wide is it? 31,518 miles (50,724 km)
What is its average surface temperature? −320°F (−195°C)
Where is it in the solar system? Seventh closest to the Sun
What type of planet is it? Ice giant; rings
Why is it special? It's the only planet with a unique tilt (98 degrees).

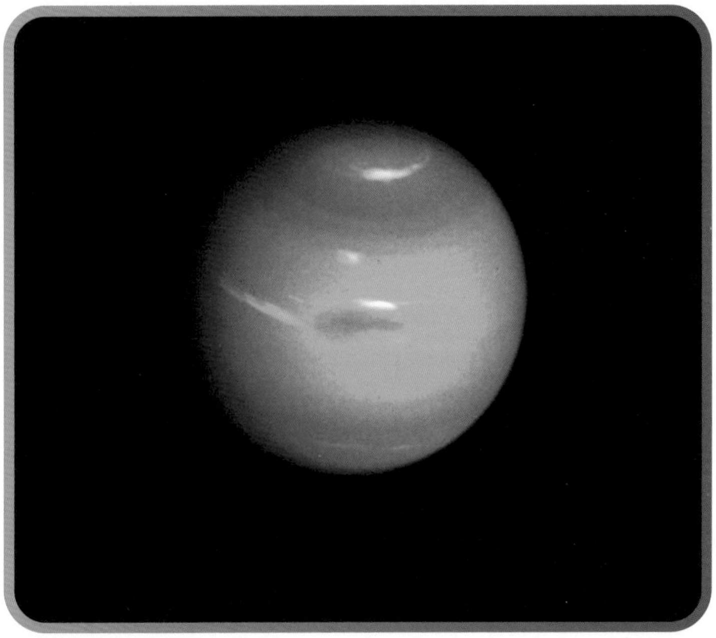

Neptune

How wide is it? 30,599 miles (49,244 km)
What is its average surface temperature? −331°F (−201°C)
Where is it in the solar system? Farthest from the Sun
What type of planet is it? Ice giant; rings
Why is it special? It's the only planet that is never visible to the naked eye.

*NASA, 2021

GAZING INTO SPACE

What is it like to live on the INTERNATIONAL SPACE STATION?

The current space station has been in operation since 2000, with visits by astronauts from 15 nations. It travels 5 miles (8 km) per second and orbits Earth 16 times a day. The rotating crew of six spends most of its time maintaining the station and conducting scientific research. The astronauts have to eat, sleep, exercise, and use the toilet too, of course. (There are two space bathrooms to choose from.) They eat a variety of food, often rehydrated. Each sleeping quarter is about the size of a phone booth. Crew members use sleeping bags that tie down to prevent drifting in low gravity, and facemasks to keep out the sunlight. They exercise at least two hours a day in the space gym to maintain muscle and bone mass. At dawn or dusk, you might be able to see the International Space Station in the sky for yourself. After all, it is 356 feet (109 m) long—almost the full length of a football field.

Learn More

Go to the National Aeronautics and Space Administration to see short videos about its latest activities and research. You can also track the International Space Station from there.

- www.nasa.gov/videos

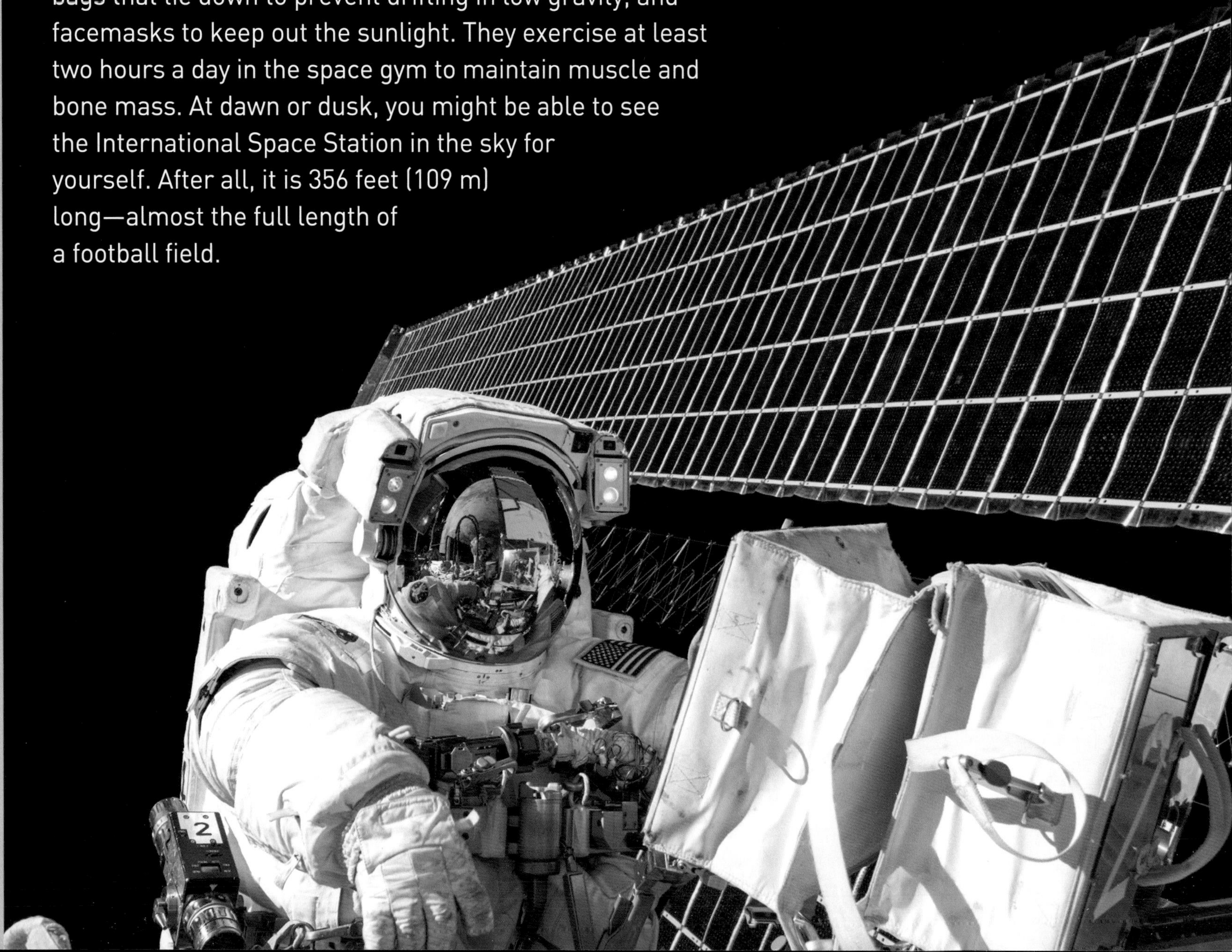

Q&A: A Remarkable Person

Mae Jemison

Astronaut and Physician

When and where was she born? 1956, in Decatur, Alabama

What did she tell her kindergarten teacher she wanted to be when she grew up? A scientist, a dancer, an architect, and a fashion designer

What did she do after becoming a physician? Served as a medical officer with the Peace Corps in Sierra Leone and Liberia (1983)

What has she accomplished? Became the first Black woman in space, on the space shuttle *Endeavour* (1992)

What has she said? "I realized I would feel comfortable anywhere in the universe because I belonged to and was a part of it, as much as any star, planet, asteroid, comet, or nebula."

What are NASA ASTRONAUTS not allowed to EAT in space?

Salt and pepper (the seasonings would just float around so they use a liquid version), soda (it causes digestive discomfort), fish (it's too pungent), or chips (they are not healthy enough, and might produce crumbs that interfere with sensitive equipment).

How do we know EARTH ISN'T FLAT?

You mean in addition to all of our scientific knowledge—and pictures of our round planet taken from space? One simple way to prove it, carried out more than 2,000 years ago by ancient Greeks, involves sticks. If Earth were flat, with the Sun directly overhead, a vertical stick would cast the same shadow as another stick several hundred miles north. But it doesn't. Why? Because Earth is curved.

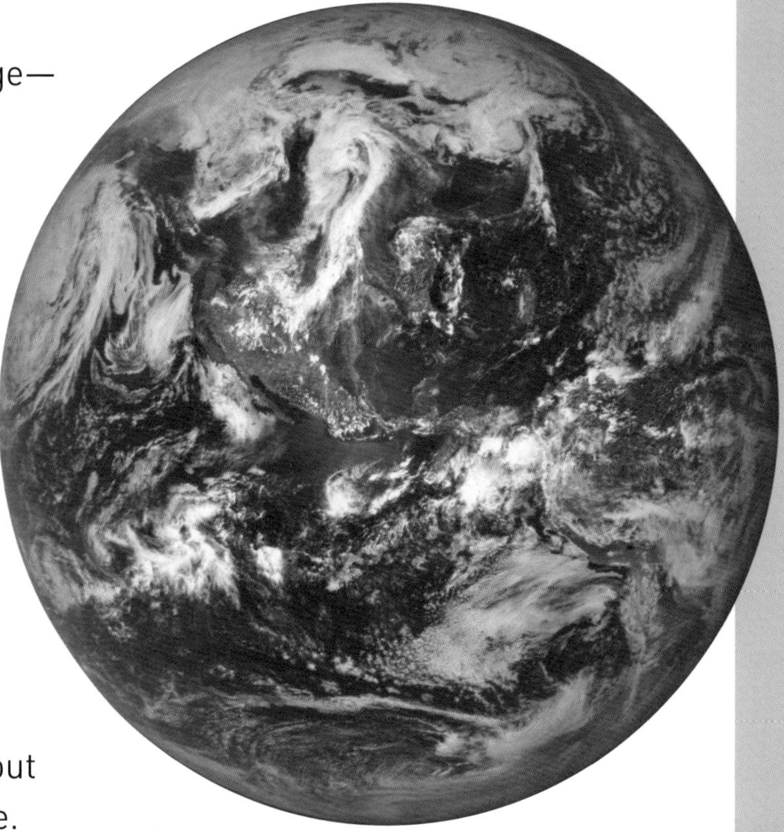

Why does NASA study EARTH?

It might seem funny that the National Aeronautics and Space Administration would study its own planet. In fact, Earth is the planet that NASA has explored the most. Its satellites and telescopes are helping researchers learn more about all kinds of Earthly things, including climate change.

SPACING OUT

What is the difference between a METEOR and a METEORITE?

Look! A light quickly streaks through the night sky. You may have just seen a "shooting star." But it is not an actual star. It is a meteor—a small chunk of rock that hits Earth's atmosphere and burns up, glowing as it travels. Stargazers might see one every 15 minutes—more during meteor showers. If that chunk survives its fiery fall and lands on Earth's surface, it's known as a meteorite. Earth gets an estimated 500 meteorites each year. Most fall into the ocean or in remote areas of the world. Fewer than 10 are actually recovered.

Is there LIFE on OTHER PLANETS?

There is no yes-or-no answer to this question. Take ALH 84001. Snowmobiling scientists discovered this space rock in Antarctica in 1984. They believe the rock—shaped like a large potato—formed on Mars four billion years ago and landed on Earth about 13,000 years ago. Then, in 1996, NASA researchers announced possible signs of life in the rock potato. Many say the clue (a fossil) isn't enough evidence of life on Mars. Debate continues to this day. But scientific discovery can further knowledge without being conclusive. NASA recently suggested a framework to evaluate deep-space finds like ALH 84001. The seven-level scale would help provide a working definition of "life" based on astrobiology, the study of life outside Earth.

How are COMETS like SNOWBALLS?

Like snowballs, comets are frozen pieces of ice. Unlike snowballs, comets orbit the Sun. They consist of ice, rocks, dust, and gas and are miles wide. Scientists believe comets are leftover material from the formation of the solar system. When a comet moves closer to the Sun, the ice melts and boils off. The glowing head of a comet can be larger than a planet, with a tail that stretches millions of miles.

Q&A: A Remarkable Person

Stephen Hawking

Cosmologist

When and where was he born? 1942, in Oxford, England (he died in 2018)

What were his childhood hobbies? Raising bees in the basement and producing fireworks in the greenhouse

What major life event happened when he was 21 years old? Was diagnosed with amyotrophic lateral sclerosis (ALS), a neuromuscular disease that causes paralysis, with doctors saying he had just two years to live

What did he accomplish? Proposed theories that help explain black holes, gravity, and the big bang

What did he say? "Remember to look up at the stars and not down at your feet. Try to make sense of what you see and wonder about what makes the universe exist. Be curious."

How do BLACK HOLES form?

When a large star dies, or uses up its fuel, a black hole can form. A black hole is an area in space where gravity is so strong that not even light can escape it. Matter has been squeezed down to a tiny point called a singularity. Black holes can be small or supermassive. Oh, and they're not black at all. They are invisible. They lie at the center of most galaxies. Scientists believe the smallest black holes formed when the universe began.

Learn More

Go to the American Museum of Natural History for stargazing tips.

- www.amnh.org/explore/ology/astronomy/a-kids-guide-to-stargazing

A NUMBERS GAME

How DEEP is the OCEAN?

The deepest part of the ocean is the Challenger Deep in the Pacific Ocean's Mariana Trench. It is about 36,200 feet (11,034 m) deep. If it were possible to place Mount Everest at the bottom of the trench, its peak would still be more than a mile (1.6 km) underwater. That's deep.

What is the OLDEST LIVING THING on Earth?

To answer this question, you need to define "living thing." If you don't count clonal organisms—life that comes from a single ancestor, like seagrass—the answer is a tree in California's White Mountains. A bristlecone pine named Methuselah would have more than 5,000 candles on its birthday cake, if trees had birthday parties.

Why isn't a YEAR always 365 DAYS?

Earth moves around the Sun once every 365.25 days. It is called a solar year. So every four calendar years, we have one extra day. To make up for that, the calendar year adds a day every four years. In so-called leap years, February has 29 days instead of 28. Without this correction, eventually, we would be shoveling snow in July.

Q&A: A Remarkable Person

Katherine Johnson

NASA Mathematician

When and where was she born? 1918, White Sulphur Springs, West Virginia (she died in 2020)

When did she start high school? When she was 10

What did she accomplish? Calculated flight paths for the NASA missions that put astronaut John Glenn into orbit around Earth (1962) and sent the first three astronauts to the Moon (1969)

What is the highest honor she received? Presidential Medal of Freedom, the highest American civilian honor, for her contributions as one of the first Black women to work as a NASA scientist (2015)

What did she say? "Everything was so new—the whole idea of going into space was new and daring. There were no textbooks, so we had to write them."

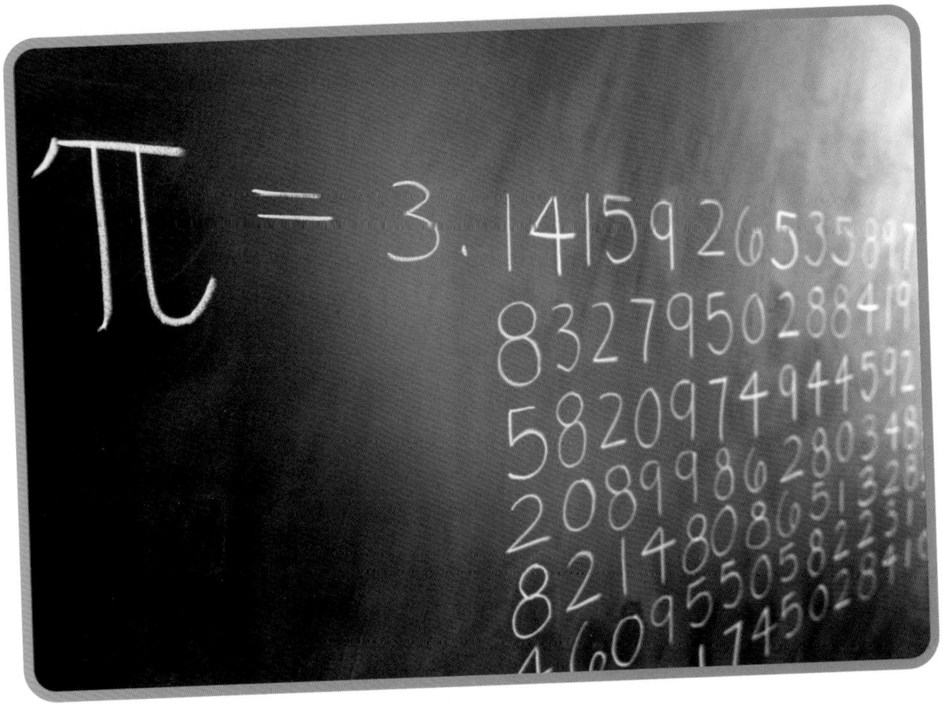

Is MATH invented or discovered?

Mathematical equations are like sentences that explain patterns. But mathematicians question whether they are there for us to discover or whether we invent them to explain the world around us. Either way, math is a wonder.

Why is it called PI? (What is PI?)

Pi equals a number close to 3.14. But that number goes on forever; it's infinite. So what is pi? Pi is the circumference of a circle (the distance around it) divided by the diameter (the distance of a line drawn straight across it). That means the distance around any circle is about 3.14 times the width. We use pi to find any circle's area and circumference. That can be useful as there are so many circles in nature. In 1706, the Welsh mathematician William Jones gave pi its name, written as the Greek letter for *p*, or π. It is the first letter in the Greek word *perimitros*, or "perimeter." Math lovers celebrate March 14, or 3/14, as Pi Day. Get it?

FULL S.T.E.M. AHEAD

What do we know about the very BOTTOM of the OCEAN?

Very little, in fact. Much of the ocean floor is still a mystery. About 80 percent of it has never been surveyed. An international project is underway to map the global seabed by 2030. Animals and plants have had to adapt to cold temperatures and intense pressure to live here. Researchers believe their chemical compounds could help fight human disease. Further study of the deep sea might lead to more renewable energy. The ocean could even play a role in countering climate change.

Learn More

Go to Ocean Exploration at the National Oceanic Atmospheric Administration to see daily images of the deep sea.

- oceanexplorer.noaa.gov/multimedia/daily-image

Q&A: A Remarkable Person

Sylvia Earle

Oceanographer

When and where was she born? 1935, in Gibbstown, New Jersey

When did she first become fascinated by the ocean? When she was knocked over by a wave as a little girl

What has she accomplished? Led more than 100 ocean expeditions, logged more than 7,000 hours underwater, and wrote more than 100 scientific papers

What else has she accomplished? Holds the world record for the deepest untethered sea walk at 1,250 feet (381 m) (1979)

What has she said? "Go see the ocean for yourself and use your talents whatever they are to make a difference for yourself and for the natural world, because it all ties together."

Could Harry Potter's **CLOAK OF INVISIBILITY** exist in the future?

Just think. Nanoscience is the study of extremely small things. (A nanometer is one billionth of a meter.) Imagine studying something 1,000 times smaller than the width of a human hair. That is, at the scale of atoms, the atomic level. You might use your knowledge of nanoscience to create a unique material. Then, throwing on a Harry Potter space-time cape to hide might not be as unimaginable as you think.

Why isn't it called **COVID-20**?

COVID-19 is short for *coronavirus disease 2019*. The *CO* in COVID-19 stands for "corona." *VI* stands for "virus," and *D* is short for "disease." On February 11, 2020, the World Health Organization announced the official name of the disease, first identified in December 2019.

Why isn't there a **CURE** for the **COMMON COLD**?

Too many types of viruses—at least 200—can cause colds. And they mutate too quickly. By the time a vaccine was developed, it would no longer be useful. A bowl of hot soup and rest is still the way to go. Also, cough or sneeze into your elbow, wash your hands, and try to avoid close contact with other people if you're feeling sick.

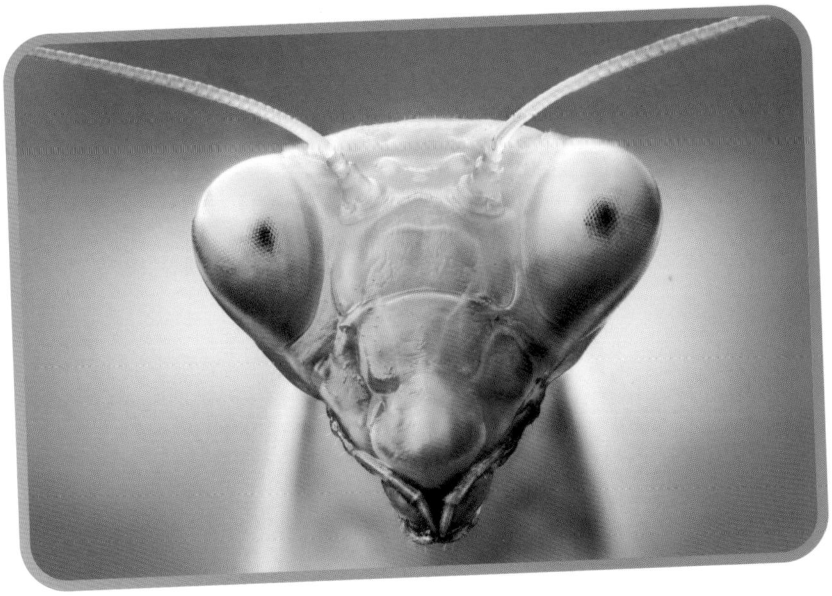

What **ANIMALS** are likely to **TAKE OVER** a future world?

For fun, a few American biologists answered this still very theoretical question. Rats, cockroaches, and pigeons (they are thriving already in cities). Termites (they would adapt to digest plastic). Giant bugs (they would grow as large as dogs in an oxygen-rich world). Merely guesses. But a little terrifying all the same, right?

SPORTS

There are many ways to play sports. You can throw and catch, dribble and shoot, pitch and hit, serve and return. You can dive, stick the landing, make a save. You can play at the highest levels in the world. You can play for your school. You can play just for fun. Being a spectator is thrilling too. What is the oldest team sport in North America? How many people does it take to start a wave? Why do you wear a gi in karate? Are you game for some answers? On your mark, get set, go!

FOOTBALLING

What is the most popular American SPECTATOR SPORT?

In one survey, football tackled first place (37 percent). Basketball rebounded in second (11 percent), followed by baseball and softball (9 percent). Stepping up next was soccer (7 percent). Ice hockey slid into fifth place (4 percent). The percentage of Americans without any favorite sport was up (15 percent). How can that be?

Why are footballs SHAPED like that?

Footballs used to be made of inflated pig bladders, which are somewhat oval in shape. It's gross but true. As the sport developed into more of a passing than kicking game, the ball gained pointy ends that made it easier to carry and throw. That's how a football got its unusual shape. It's called a prolate spheroid, by the way.

Why is the NFL's "Big Game" called the SUPER BOWL?

The American Football League (AFL) and National Football League (NFL) merged in 1966. Their final contest first used a not-so-catchy name—the AFL-NFL World Championship Game. Then a new name caught on, inspired by a bouncy ball toy that AFL founder Lamar Hunt's children played with called a Super Ball.

Learn More

Go to the Pro Football Hall of Fame for the history of your favorite team.

- www.profootballhof.com

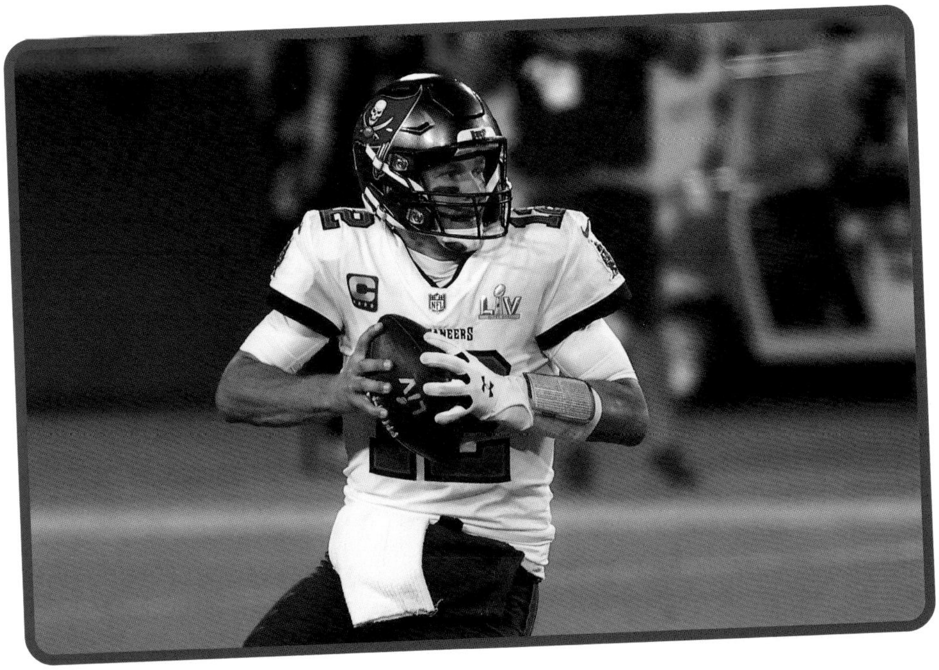

Why is it called a SACK?

Bringing down the quarterback with the ball behind the line of scrimmage used to be called "tackling the QB for a loss." In the 1960s, NFL defensive lineman Deacon Jones dubbed the practice a sack. (Ancient armies conquered, or sacked, lands.) "Sacking a quarterback," Jones explained, "is just like you devastate a city."

Where does the word SOCCER come from?

In most English-speaking countries, the sport that Americans know as *soccer* is called football. It might be surprising to learn the word soccer has British origins. In 1863, the Football Association in London, England, wrote a set of rules for the modern game. They named it *association football*. Since that's a mouthful, the name of the sport was often shortened to "assoc," then "soc," and also "soccer," or "socker." Or just football. But in countries with other forms of football, like the United States, Canada, and Australia, the name *soccer* stuck.

Q&A: A Remarkable Person

Carli Lloyd

Soccer Player

When and where was she born? 1984, in Delran, New Jersey

What sports did she play as a kid? Roller hockey, football, basketball, softball, volleyball, swimming, and soccer

What has she accomplished? Won two FIFA World Cups (2015, 2019) and two Olympic gold medals (2008, 2012)

What else has she accomplished? Was named FIFA World Player of the Year (2015, 2016)

What has she said? "Playing in Wembley Stadium in front of 83-some-thousand fans to win a gold medal was unreal. I think, male or female, that was a record number."

LET'S PLAY BALL

Is it true that basketball was first played with REAL BASKETS?

Yes, a gym teacher named James Naismith invented the game with two discarded peach baskets—and a soccer ball. On December 21, 1891, in Springfield, Massachusetts, Naismith introduced "basket ball" to his students. Players could not run with the ball—they could only pass it. (Dribbling was added later.) Baskets were "goals," and there were two 15-minute halves. In the first game, players managed to score just one "goal," but it turned out to be fun indoor exercise on a winter day. Today, more than 300 million people play basketball worldwide, indoors or out.

Learn More

Go to the Naismith Memorial Basketball Hall of Fame to see the men and women inductees.

- www.hoophall.com

How did baseball get NINE INNINGS?

Baseball games used to last until one team scored 21 runs. This took about six innings in the 1840s. But baseball pitching improved through the years. That made it harder to score and much longer to complete games. By 1856, many games were being called due to darkness. No stadium lights back then! A change was needed. Organizers met to choose between seven or nine innings—and players on each team. Preferring a more competitive defense, they opted for the larger number.

Why do baseball players sit in DUGOUTS?

Players used to just sit on benches when they weren't on the field or up to bat. Low shelters called dugouts became part of the professional game by 1908. Putting the players below the field level allowed spectators a better view of the action at home plate. Ballpark dugouts ensure the best seats go to fans—the people who bought tickets.

What is the OLDEST TEAM SPORT in North America?

Lacrosse. The fast-paced sport in which players use sticks with nets on the end to pass a ball and score has Indigenous origins in North America, where the game was first played more than 500 years ago. The games, major events set up across villages, could last for days. The Algonquin called it *baggataway*. The Iroquois named it *tewaarathon*. French settlers gave it the name lacrosse, after the sticks that looked like a Catholic bishop's staff, or *crosier*.

Q&A: A Remarkable Person

LeBron James

Basketball Player

When and where was he born? 1984, in Akron, Ohio

When did he first start playing organized basketball? In fifth grade

What has he accomplished? Won four NBA championships and four NBA Finals MVP Awards (2012, 2013, 2016, 2020)

What else has he accomplished? Helped open a public school (2018) in Akron supported by the LeBron James Family Foundation (2004)

What has he said? "Once you become a professional athlete or once you do anything well, then you're automatically a role model. . . I have no problem being a role model, I love it. I have kids looking up to me and hopefully I inspire these kids to do good things."

TOP OF THE PODIUM

Why do Olympic athletes BITE THEIR MEDALS?

Gold winners used to bite down on the medal to test the metal. Real gold is softer than many other metals and shows teeth marks. But Olympic medals haven't been solid gold since the games in Stockholm, Sweden, in 1912. Now, they are mostly silver, coated with 0.2 ounces (6 g) of gold. Medals at the 2020 Tokyo Olympics came from recycled electronics donated by the Japanese public. Today, most images of athletes on the podium chomping their prize are just a fun tradition.

Where did the FIVE OLYMPIC RINGS come from?

Pierre de Coubertin, the French founder of the modern Olympics, created the interlocking rings to represent five continents. He drew them by hand on the top of a letter in 1913 and colored them blue, yellow, green, red, and black. Did you know it is possible to reproduce the flag of every country in the world with these colors?

Why is there a new Olympic MOTTO?

In 2021, the International Olympic Committee added one word to the organization's original motto. The new motto is: *Citius, Altius, Fortius – Communiter*, or Faster, Higher, Stronger – Together. The addition of the word "together" recognizes the power of sport and the importance of solidarity.

Make a Difference

Be the leader of a fun outdoor game with neighbors or friends. Ask what they would most enjoy playing. Organize the time and location. Sometimes playing, not winning, is everything.

THE WHYS BEHIND THE OLYMPICS, PARALYMPICS, AND SPECIAL OLYMPICS

All three organizations hold international events every two years, alternating in summer and winter. The Special Olympics also offer training and smaller contests year-round.

Olympics

For whom? Best non-disabled athletes in the world
Why? To compete at the highest levels
How many countries participate? More than 200
Since when? 1896
Where does the name come from? Olympia, the small Greek town where sporting contests first honored the Greek god Zeus 3,000 years ago

Learn More

Go to the Olympics, Paralympics, and Special Olympics for highlights and history.

- olympics.com
- www.paralympic.org
- www.specialolympics.org

Paralympics

For whom? Best athletes in the world with disabilities
Why? To compete at the highest levels
How many countries participate? More than 160
Since when? 1960
What does the name mean? An event parallel with the Olympics (*para* means "beside" in Greek)

Special Olympics World Games

For whom? Those from age eight and up with an intellectual disability, of all skill levels
Why? To learn and play sports in a safe environment
How many countries participate? More than 170
Since when? 1968
Who founded it? Eunice Kennedy Shriver, sister of President John F. Kennedy, who ran a summer camp in 1962 for children with intellectual disabilities

SPLASHDOWN

Why do DIVERS take SHOWERS between dives and towel off while competing?

It's all about keeping muscles loose and skin dry. The water in a diving pool—and the air when you're wet—is cold. The warm shower water helps keep the diver's body warm and muscles loose, reducing the chance of a muscle pull or strain. And goose bumps. Divers also cannot afford slippery hands or legs during a pike or tuck in the air. They use little towels called chamois (pronounced "shammy") to dry off quickly between dives.

Why do swimmers wear TWO CAPS for races?

Putting on a second cap can help keep your goggles in place during a race. That seems practical enough. The other reason is more technical. The second cap, usually silicone, doesn't wrinkle, which helps reduce drag. Drag is the resistance the water exerts on your body as you move through it. It seems to work for Olympic swimming champion Katie Ledecky!

Why do SYNCHRONIZED SWIMMERS wear nose clips?

Did you know that swimmers sometimes spend up to half of their routine underwater? So those little devices pinch the nostrils closed. That prevents water from entering the nasal cavity during the upside-down movements. Swimmers carry a spare in their swimsuits in case it gets knocked off during the complex routines.

Is there a difference between ROWING and CREW?

No. Crew is what U.S. high schools and colleges call the sport of rowing. In rowing, or sweep rowing, there are boats of two, four, or eight athletes. They all row together, each with one oar. When an athlete rows with two oars, it's called sculling. In sculling, there are singles, pairs, and quads. A coxswain, who must be light, sits in the boat and calls out instructions to the rowers.

How did SURFING become an Olympic sport?

Sports must be widely practiced by a number of countries and on at least three continents to qualify as an event in the Olympic Games. They must contribute to the "value and appeal" of the Olympics and reflect its traditions. In 2020, organizers were focused on youth and attracting new fans. That might be why surfing—along with karate, skateboarding, and sport climbing—debuted at the Tokyo Olympics.

Q&A: A Remarkable Person

Carissa Moore

Professional Surfer

When and where was she born? 1992, in Honolulu, Hawaii

When did she start surfing? When she was about five, with her father, at Waikiki Beach

How does she overcome nerves before matches? Takes a deep breath and thinks of a positive image or memory

What has she accomplished? Won five World Surf League titles (2011, 2013, 2015, 2019, 2021) and an Olympic gold medal (2021)

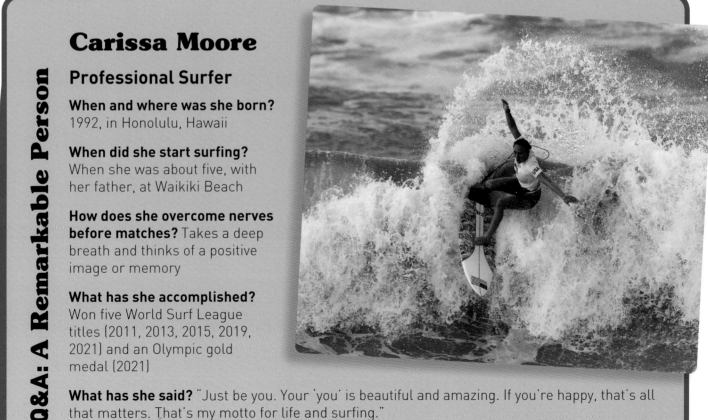

What has she said? "Just be you. Your 'you' is beautiful and amazing. If you're happy, that's all that matters. That's my motto for life and surfing."

WHAT A RACKET!

Who invented PICKLEBALL? How did the game get that name?

Pickleball started in western United States, on Bainbridge Island, Washington. Three dads invented it in 1965 to entertain their children, restless during the summer. It's now the country's fastest-growing sport. The simple game has been called a mash-up of tennis, badminton, and Ping-Pong. It requires a paddle, a plastic ball with holes, a net, a court, and an opponent. You can play singles or doubles, indoors or outdoors. One story says pickleball is named after a cocker spaniel owned by one of the inventors. He kept stealing the ball.

Learn More

Go to the Official USA Pickleball Places 2 Play to find a location to play near you.

- www.places2play.org

Why is it called BADMINTON?

Badminton was named after the country estate of the dukes of Beaufort in Gloucestershire, England. That's where the lawn game was first played in about 1873. All it requires is a net, light, long-handled rackets, a shuttlecock, also called a birdie. And an underhand serve.

Why is 6–0 in a set of tennis called "SIX-LOVE"?

Tennis has used the word *love*—meaning one player has not yet won a game in a set—since the late 1800s. Some say it relates to the sport's origins in 12th-century France. *L'oeuf* is the French word for "the egg," which looks a lot like zero and sounds a bit like "love." It may be clever reasoning, but the French don't use the word *l'oeuf* to mean zero. So there's a better explanation. And that is: if you didn't win a single game in the set, you are playing for the "love of the game." Isn't that a love-ly thought?

Q&A: A Remarkable Person

Naomi Osaka

Tennis Player

When and where was she born? 1997, in Osaka, Japan

When did she move to the United States and start playing tennis? When she was three

How old was she when she became a professional tennis player? 15

What has she accomplished? Became the first Japanese player to win a singles title in a Grand Slam (U.S. Open, 2018) and the first Asian player to be ranked number one in the world

What has she said? "I've been always following people . . . following blueprints of people. And now I feel like I didn't really find or . . . see a lane or a path that I liked, and I was at a standstill. And then I found that you have to make your own path."

Why are TENNIS BALLS yellow?

Two words: color television. In 1972, the International Tennis Federation approved the use of yellow balls. They were easier to see during televised matches than the traditional white ones. Wimbledon, however, did not adopt the familiar neon color until 1986.

SPORTY LOOKS

Why must **TENNIS PLAYERS** dress in white at **WIMBLEDON?**

The Wimbledon Championships in England is the world's oldest tennis tournament. Its dress code was written in the 1880s. All players must be "dressed in suitable tennis attire that is almost entirely in white." Back then, it was considered improper for athletes to perspire on their clothes. And it was thought that white clothes would be cooler and that any sweat would be harder to see on white clothes than on colorful fabrics. Even footwear must be white at Wimbledon. Roger Federer, the record holder for the most Wimbledon men's singles titles—eight!—was told not to wear his orange-soled sneakers again on the court in 2013.

Why do **BASKETBALL** players wear **TIGHTS?**

NBA teams usually play 82 games a season. Players do everything they can to stay healthy. That might include racing up and down the court in short, knee-length, or full-length compression tights. The often-stylish leggings provide protection between skin and the court. Some pros even wear them with padding. The tights help increase blood flow, therefore performance. They also reduce the risk of harm, as warmer muscles mean fewer injuries.

Why do SOCCER PLAYERS swap shirts?

Trading jerseys after a game is a sign of respect between two players. They are usually of a similar skill level. The swapping ritual took place first in 1931, after France beat England for the first time in an international game. The French players were so overjoyed, they asked for England's shirts as mementos. The English agreed.

Why do you wear a gi in KARATE?

Gi is Japanese for "uniform." It's short for *karategi*. (*Karate* means "empty hand" in Japanese.) The gi, white with shortened sleeves and pants, allows free movement. Your first belt is customarily in white. The colored belts represent levels of achievement in the sport. After white, they are usually yellow, orange, green, blue, brown, and black in color. Originally, the white belt was simply dyed to a new color, and the colors grew increasingly darker.

Why do REFEREES wear black and white stripes?

In the early days of football, officials wore formal clothes. A white dress shirt and a bow tie conveyed authority to the coaches and players. But when a team wore white too, a problem cropped up—mistaken identity. In 1920, a quarterback accidentally passed the ball to the game's referee. That referee, named Lloyd Olds, was perturbed and came up with a solution: black and white stripes. He wore his specially made shirt to ref the 1921 Michigan state high school basketball championships. The distinctive look quickly caught on across the country.

N(ICE) GAMES

Why are HOCKEY PUCKS frozen?

Freezing a rubber hockey puck keeps it from bouncing on the ice. A frozen puck is easier for players to control. Pucks thaw quickly, however. National Hockey League officials replace them—from a portable freezer—throughout the game.

Learn More

Go to the National Hockey League for scores, videos, and a list of the 100 greatest players.

- www.nhl.com

Why is scoring three goals in a single game called a HAT TRICK?

An impressive feat is called a trick. The expression "hat trick" started with the English game of cricket. In 1858, a cricket player took three wickets with consecutive balls. Which is incredible, provided you understand the rules of cricket. The cricket club did, of course, and rewarded him for his achievement with a bowler hat. According to the Hockey Hall of Fame, in the 1940s, a Canadian haberdasher gave free fedoras to any professional player who scored three goals in a single game. You have to play well to look good.

What's the difference between ICE DANCING and PAIRS SKATING?

Two skaters are on the ice. Check. But which event are they competing in? Well, if it looks a little like gymnastics on ice, it's pairs skating. If it looks more like a ballroom dancing competition, ice dancing is a better bet. Another clue that you're watching ice dancing is synchronized turns on one foot, called twizzles. In pairs skating, you'll see lifts, side-by-side jumps, throw jumps, and death spirals. Yikes.

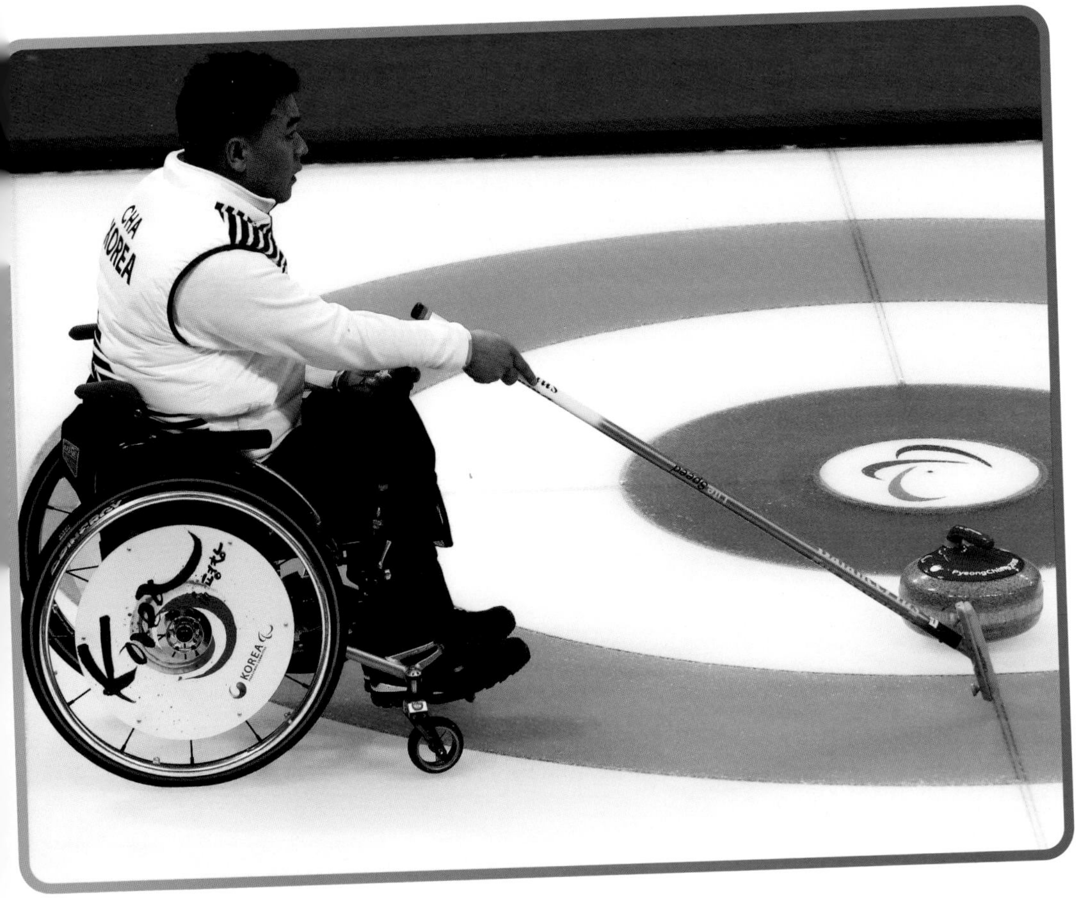

What is CURLING?

Curling, like hockey, is a team sport played on ice. The similarities pretty much end there. In this Olympic and Paralympic sport, two teams take turns sliding granite stones on a long stretch of ice. The goal is to land on the target circle called a house. There are four players, or curlers, per team. Curlers help the stone move where they want it by furiously sweeping the ice in front of it with a broom. In addition to broom skills, strategy and patience are required to win. Unlike hockey, this game has been called "chess on ice."

Q&A: A Remarkable Person

Mikaela Shiffrin

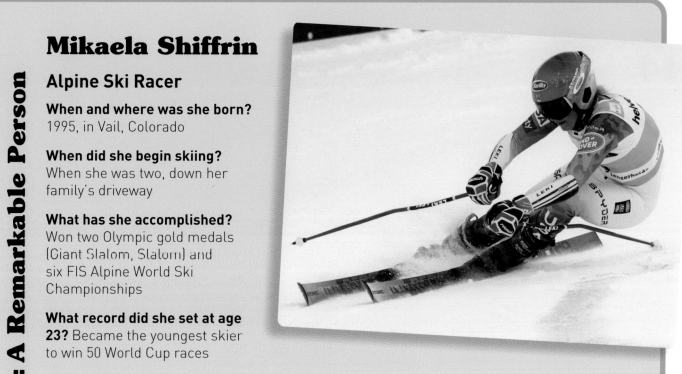

Alpine Ski Racer

When and where was she born? 1995, in Vail, Colorado

When did she begin skiing? When she was two, down her family's driveway

What has she accomplished? Won two Olympic gold medals (Giant Slalom, Slalom) and six FIS Alpine World Ski Championships

What record did she set at age 23? Became the youngest skier to win 50 World Cup races

What has she said? "If you strive toward the perfect run, accepting that you will always come up short of that is very intriguing. It makes me think about how in life in general, we always want to strive toward perfection, but sometimes perfection would be the worst thing."

FAN THE GAMES

How many people does it take to START A WAVE?

This spur-of-the-moment, yet coordinated, activity of standing, throwing hands in the air, and quickly sitting down again is a crowd-pleaser at sports events. According to a scientific study, it takes only about 20 to 35 people to trigger a wave. Stadium waves typically move clockwise at a speed of about 20 seats per second. Participants must be spread out in the stands, in both the top and bottom rows. The mood of the crowd is key. Waves tend to occur most often during the slow moments of a game. Or when fans are enthusiastic—everyone likes to stretch and cheer when their team is winning.

Why do SPORTS TEAMS have MASCOTS?

These larger-than-life characters bring fans to their feet to cheer the team on. Before a Padres game in 1979, the San Diego Chicken famously hatched out of a 10-foot (3-m) egg. The "birth" was even covered on live TV. For professional teams, a mascot helps promote their sponsors. And mascots appear at college and high school games to boost school spirit. At any level, a furry—or feathered—mascot entertains fans, especially the youngest ones, during lopsided games and pauses in the action.

Why do INDIANAPOLIS 500 winners drink MILK when they win?

The peculiar tradition started in 1933 with the race car driver Louis Meyer. Apparently, his mother told him as a child to drink buttermilk when thirsty. After taking the checkered flag in the Indy 500, Meyer requested a glass, and photos captured him swilling buttermilk. Three years later, when Meyer won again, his buttermilk appeared in a fancy glass bottle. The Milk Foundation had seen a marketing opportunity. Since 1956, the winning driver has been awarded a bottle of milk after the grueling race. Sometimes they even pour the cold milk over their heads. Only once did a driver refuse to participate in the tradition. He asked for orange juice. Crowds booed him at the next race.

Why do sports teams move to DIFFERENT CITIES?

The Los Angeles Lakers were originally from Minneapolis (better known for its lakes than Los Angeles). The Utah Jazz debuted in New Orleans (that one makes sense, too). In baseball, the Oakland Athletics, founded in Philadelphia in 1901, moved to Kansas City in 1955 and ended up in California in 1968. But when the Raiders moved to Las Vegas in 2020, Oakland lost its football team. Owners relocate their teams in a search for bigger profits, tax breaks, better facilities, and stronger fan support. So cheer your teams on!

What Are the All-Time Most-Watched SPORTING EVENTS?*

EVENT	ESTIMATED TV VIEWERSHIP
Summer Olympics (2012, 2016)	3.60 billion
FIFA World Cup (2018)	3.57 billion
Tour de France (2019)	3.5 billion
Cricket World Cup (2019)	2.2 billion
Winter Olympics (2006)	2.1 billion

*Stadium Talk, 2021

TECH UP

Technology is the invention and use of tools or techniques to solve problems. It could be something you can touch, like a smartphone, or something you can't, like artificial intelligence. New technologies are all around us. They help us fly through the sky safely, perform delicate surgeries, and communicate around the world in split seconds. What was the earliest technology? Why is malware dangerous? What causes traffic jams? Will robots make my bed for me anytime soon? Time to tech up.

@HOME

What was the EARLIEST TECHNOLOGY?

About two million years ago, early humans chipped away at pieces of stone to create a chopping tool. That tool could lop off tree branches and cut animal meat. One of those simple stone tools was found in Tanzania and is now on display at the British Museum. It was the earliest technological invention.

Make a Difference

Check in with older family members or neighbors who may need help programming their devices at home.

What are SMART TOILETS?

You know about smartphones, but what about smart toilets? In addition to a heated seat, an automatic lid, and a nightlight, a high-tech toilet can clean (and dry) your body—and itself. A smart toilet saves water by using only as much as is needed. Isn't that clever? The smart toilet of the future may even share real-time data of what you produce with your doctor to track illness.

How does a ROBOTIC VACUUM CLEANER work?

The machine glides along, seemingly with a mind of its own. When its whirring and rotations are over, a spotless floor remains. While the early machines moved randomly, some newer models use navigation software. They map each room so no spot is missed. Mechanical or infrared sensors detect carpet, furniture, and walls. A brush roller and suction power remove dirt, collected by a dustbin inside. The cordless sweeper returns on its own to its charging dock to power up for the next day.

Why does it seem as though everything is CONNECTED to the INTERNET?

In some ways, because it is! There's a name for it: the Internet of Things (IoT). At home, more and more thermostats, security systems, sprinklers, lights, refrigerators, and other devices are designed to exchange data over the internet. They are automatically controlled, usually with a smartphone app. The "thing" sends its user updates (You need more milk! says the smart fridge). It learns the daily habits of its user (Don't worry, the lights will be on when you get back!). Estimates say by 2030 about 50 billion IoT devices will be in use globally.

Q&A: A Remarkable Person

Alan Turing

Mathematician

When and where was he born? 1912, in London, England (he died in 1954)

What influenced him as a child? Doing his own chemistry experiments and reading a popular book called *Natural Wonders Every Child Should Know*

What did he accomplish? Invented the universal Turing "machine," a computing device with unlimited information storage that was the basis for all digital computers (1936)

What else did he accomplish? Broke Germany's secret code for communication during World War II

What did he say? "Machines take me by surprise with great frequency."

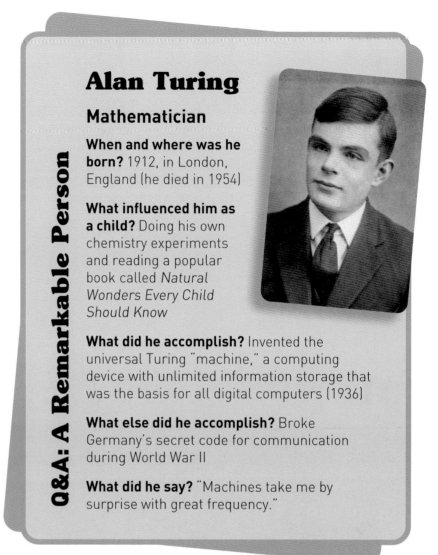

What is WI-FI short for?

The wireless technology that connects computers, smartphones, and other devices to the internet is called Wi-Fi. It uses radio waves to transfer data at high speeds over short distances. Many people think Wi-Fi is short for "wireless fidelity." Well, *hi-fi* is short for "high fidelity," or high-quality sound reproduction, right? But *Wi-Fi* isn't short for anything. A marketing firm, hired by the wireless industry, came up with the term. Everyone agreed Wi-Fi was more user-friendly than its technical name—IEEE 802.11.

SAFE SETUPS

How did the computer MOUSE get its name?

The first computer mouse, built in 1964, was a small pine wood box with a red button. Two small wheels pivoted to move the cursor. The original name was "X-Y position indicator for a display system." But everyone at the Stanford University research institute where it was invented quickly called it a mouse. Was that because the box and its power cord as a tail resembled the rodent? Or because the cursor on the screen—then called CAT—seemed to chase the tailed desktop device? Eek, a mouse! It remains the most efficient pointing device for speed and accuracy.

What's the difference between HARDWARE and SOFTWARE?

Hardware are tools made of metal. Software are your favorite pjs. Just kidding! Hardware is the nuts and bolts of a computer, and software is the program that tells a computer what to do. The word *software* originally defined the instructions for electronic calculators in 1958.

Can anyone set up an EMAIL ACCOUNT?

No. In 1998, Congress passed the Children's Online Privacy Protection Act to keep websites from collecting or using personal information of users younger than 13. That's why children of those ages may not have their own email accounts without a parent's permission. Some school districts provide email accounts to their students. However, those online sites may not collect any information for commercial use.

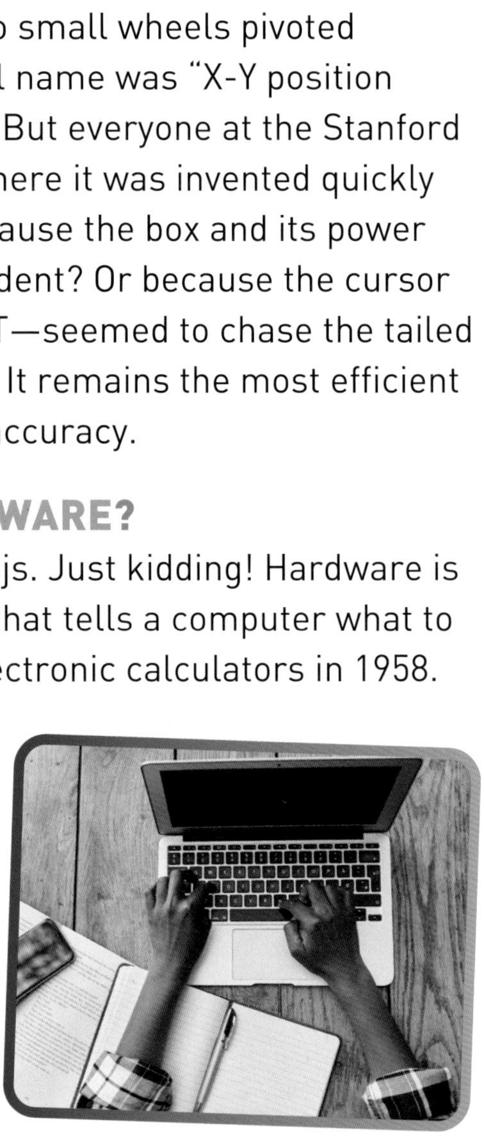

What Are the Most COMMON PASSWORDS?*

PASSWORD	NUMBER OF USERS	TIME TO CRACK IT
123456	2,543,285	Less than a second
123456789	961,435	Less than a second
picture1	371,612	3 hours
password	360,467	Less than a second

*NordPass, 2020

THE WHYS BEHIND ONLINE SAFETY*

Users of the internet can do a few things to protect themselves online. Here are the whys behind some safety tips.

Pay Attention to Updates

Why? Software updates provide up-to-date security patches (corrections to a computer program).

Don't Share Personal Information

Why? Providing information exposes the user to cyberattacks (attempts to access a computer for the purpose of causing harm or damage). That includes names, addresses, and phone numbers.

Don't Open Everything

Why? Email or attachments from unknown senders could interfere with the user's computer operations.

Use Strong Passwords

Why? Strong passwords help keep the user's personal information secure. (A strong password is a long mix of numbers, letters, and symbols.) Password generators, found online, create truly random combinations. Also, they should be changed at least a few times a year.

*Security.org, 2021

PICTURE OF HEALTH

How is a **COMPUTER VIRUS** like a real virus?

Just like a flu virus, a computer virus spreads from host to host. It attaches to a device, quickly copying itself to cause damage or steal data. Frequent crashes, slow performance, or changes to the home page are symptoms. If you do have an "infected" computer, you should "quarantine" it until an "antivirus program" is prescribed.

Why do people get **ROBOT PETS?**

A robot pet sounds like the real thing and can be soft and furry and interactive. Many even have a battery-powered heartbeat. It's no wonder they are more common than ever. Electronic pets serve as companions to elderly people or those struggling with loneliness. They can also help relieve stress, anxiety, and depression. Perhaps the biggest appeal of having a robot pet is no accidents to clean up.

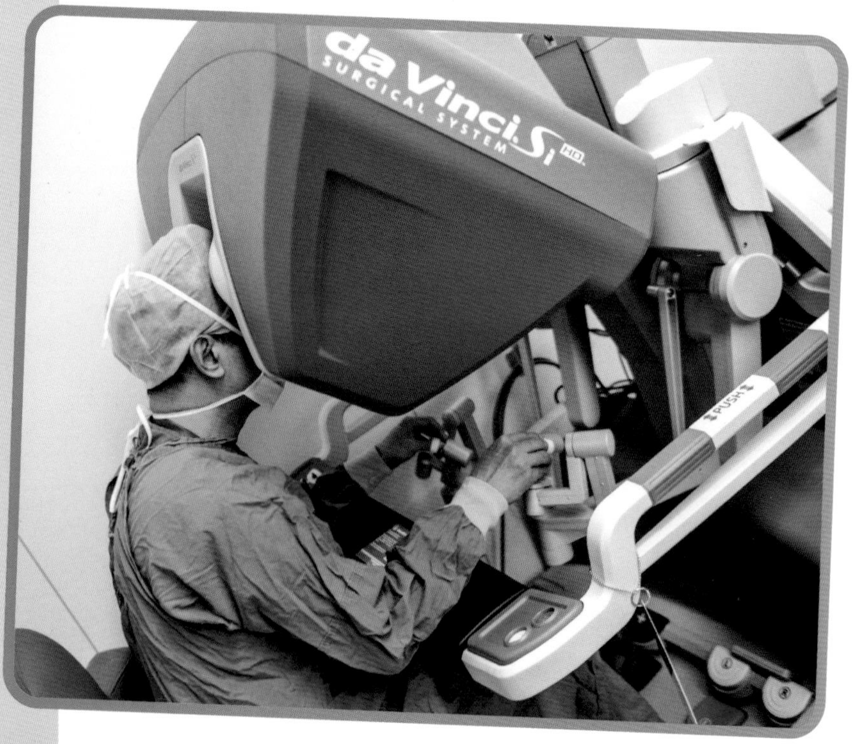

Is **ROBOTIC SURGERY** safe?

During a robotic surgery, specialized "arms" hold medical instruments and a tiny camera. The camera that's inside the patient sends real-time 3-D images to the surgeon, who sits at the console. These surgeons see images more highly magnified and at a higher resolution than they would standing directly over the patient. A robot in the operating room may sound worrisome. Yet the technology makes it possible for doctors to perform delicate surgeries in small and difficult-to-reach places of the body, with less pain and quicker recoveries for patients.

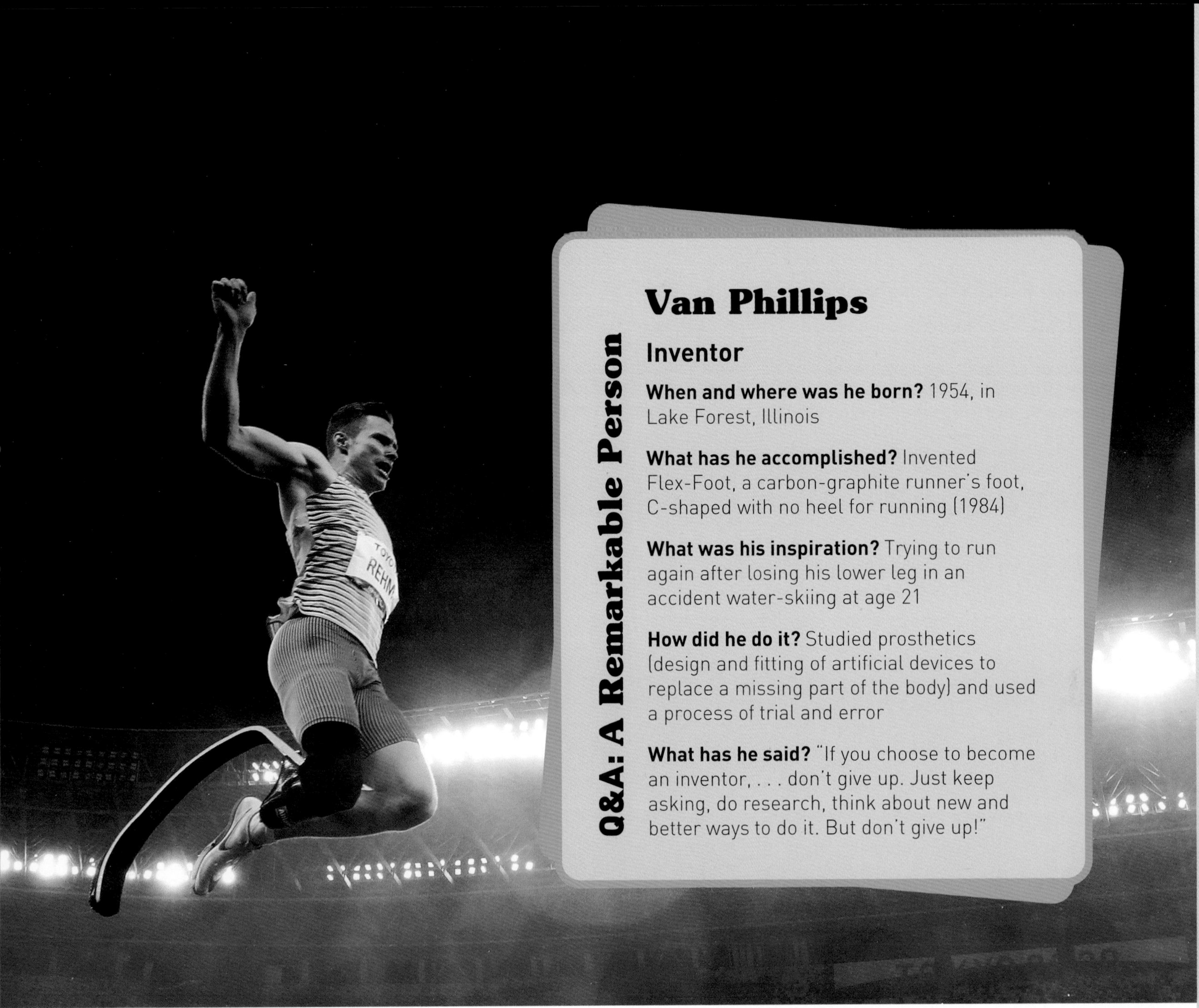

Q&A: A Remarkable Person

Van Phillips

Inventor

When and where was he born? 1954, in Lake Forest, Illinois

What has he accomplished? Invented Flex-Foot, a carbon-graphite runner's foot, C-shaped with no heel for running (1984)

What was his inspiration? Trying to run again after losing his lower leg in an accident water-skiing at age 21

How did he do it? Studied prosthetics (design and fitting of artificial devices to replace a missing part of the body) and used a process of trial and error

What has he said? "If you choose to become an inventor, . . . don't give up. Just keep asking, do research, think about new and better ways to do it. But don't give up!"

Do FITNESS TRACKERS actually improve HEALTH?

It's widely promoted that 10,000 steps a day is a good fitness goal for adults. A new report says even 7,000 daily paces makes a difference. In one study, subjects without fitness trackers lost more weight than those who wore them. No one likes to be told what to do! As for kids, they already average 10,000 to 16,000 steps a day. There is little evidence that fitness trackers increase activity levels in adolescents.

IT ALL ADDS UP

Why is MALWARE dangerous?

Beware of malware. Malware, short for "malicious software," is designed to damage or destroy computer systems. Viruses, worms (viruses that don't attach to a program), and ransomware are examples of malware. With ransomware, hackers break into computer networks and lock up data until a "ransom" is paid. This form of cybercrime can be devastating. And it's on the rise. Nearly 2,400 health-care facilities, schools, and governments in the United States were victims in 2020. Ransomware gangs stole at least $350 million.

What is CRYPTOCURRENCY?

It's money that only exists digitally. No central authority, like a country, issues "crypto." Some find excitement (or profits) investing in crypto as a new form of money, but plenty of others have lost their investments. Others use cryptocurrency to make quick payments or avoid banking fees. One can buy more than 10,000 different cryptocurrencies, including Bitcoin. Cryptocurrencies use an open, decentralized digital database called blockchain. Data is stored in encrypted batches, or blocks, chained together over time. Blockchain technology is accurate, transparent, and hard to hack. Which is good when you're talking about hard, cold e-cash.

Why do DEBIT and CREDIT CARDS now have chips?

Many criminals have learned how to steal the data from a card's magnetic stripe. The shiny microchip on the front works differently. Each time you insert your chip card in the reader, it generates a different unique code that can never be used again. That increases security and reduces fraud. Technology isn't always perfect, though, so most cards still have the stripe for swiping.

Why is it hard to COUNTERFEIT U.S. money?

Several high-tech measures make it near impossible to copy a U.S. bill. You can verify the currency in a few ways. Feel the print (it should be slightly rough). Tilt the note (some ink should change color from copper to green). Check it with light (look for a security thread woven through the bill and a watermark on both sides). And check it with magnification (look for small printed words, or microprinting). In the United States, the $20 bill is the most commonly copied banknote. Criminals elsewhere prefer to duplicate the $100 bill. For obvious reasons.

Learn More

Go to the U.S. Currency Education Program to see an illustrated timeline about the security of U.S. banknotes.

- www.uscurrency.gov/history

What are those black-and-white SQUARE CODES on everything?

Those pixelated squares you see on ads or restaurant menus are QR codes. A QR (Quick Response) code is "quickly" readable by a smartphone camera. If you look closely at one, you'll see three small squares in three corners. The camera uses them to identify the top and bottom of the code. Unlike a long barcode, a QR code holds information vertically and horizontally. That makes it faster to read. The largest QR codes measure 177 by 177 black and white dots, or modules. Anyone can generate a free QR code that links to a single website. Some businesses pay for special QR codes that track data and can be updated.

MOVING RIGHT ALONG

Why do airplanes FLY SO HIGH?

Flying at a high altitude is the most efficient way for planes to travel. The higher a plane flies, the thinner the air is. Thin air means less drag on the plane, allowing it to fly faster using less fuel. But thinner air also means less oxygen to combust with the jet fuel, which means generating less power. So the perfect cruising altitudes—not too high or too low—are usually about 30,000 feet to 40,000 feet (9,000 m to 12,000 m). Most aircraft are not approved for flight higher than 42,000 feet (13,000 m) anyway.

Learn More

Go to the Smithsonian National Air and Space Museum to explore aircraft and spacecraft in 3D.

- airandspace.si.edu/

Is it SAFER TO TRAVEL by airplane or car?

It may feel more dangerous to some, but flying in a commercial aircraft is far safer than driving in a car. Commercial flight is the safest form of transportation there is, according to the U.S. National Safety Council. Aviation technology is always improving, and planes are regularly checked for safety. Car crashes occur more often than plane crashes, though they are less likely to end up in the news. However, small private planes are less safe than flying with big commercial airlines.

What causes TRAFFIC JAMS?

Too many vehicles, poorly designed roads, traffic-light patterns, bad weather, accidents, and construction are all major causes of traffic slowdowns. But then, sometimes a phantom traffic jam pops up for no apparent reason. Any delay is a huge irritation. It starts when one car in dense traffic slows down even slightly, causing a wave of traffic behind it. The solution? One MIT researcher, inspired by flocks of flying birds, suggests keeping the same distance between you and the car in front and you and the car behind. Equal spacing of movement helps smooth out the traffic. That instruction could be added to a car's cruise controls, along with sensors for bumpers front and rear to prevent accidents. No one wants a fender bender—you know what they cause. More traffic.

Q&A: A Remarkable Person

Bessie Coleman

Aviator

When and where was she born? 1892, in Atlanta, Texas (she died in 1926)

Where did she learn how to fly? At an aviation school in Paris, France, that didn't discriminate against Black women

What has she accomplished? Became the first Black American woman and the first Native American woman to hold a pilot's license (1921)

What else has she accomplished? Performed at air shows and encouraged others to learn to fly

What did she say? "Did you know you've never lived until you've flown?"

TECHNOLOGIES, PAST AND PRESENT

What Are Some INVENTIONS of the PAST?*

Technology is always advancing. Here are the whys behind some inventions that solved practical problems in the 20th century.

Windshield Wiper

Who invented it? Mary Anderson
When? 1903
What? A rubber blade with a spring-loaded arm controlled from inside a trolley
Why? Kept trolley drivers from having to open their windows to see in bad weather. (By 1922, the automaker Cadillac had installed the wiper as standard equipment in its cars.)

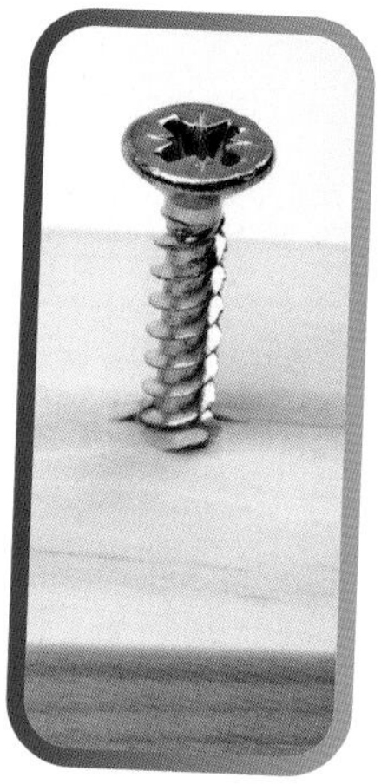

Phillips Screw

Who invented it? Henry Phillips
When? 1934
What? A self-centering screw that turns with power tools
Why? Sped up production. (By 1940, 85 percent of screw manufacturers were licensed to produce the design.)

Safety Belt

Who invented it? Nils Bohlin
When? 1959
What? A three-point seat belt in the modern automobile
Why? Secured the upper and lower body and provided one-handed buckling. (In 1959, Volvo introduced the seat belt in all its cars.)

Clean Room

Who invented it? Willis Whitfield
When? 1962
What? A room in which constantly moving air passes through filters to remove dust particles
Why? Allowed for standardized clean rooms in research divisions of government agencies such as the Department of Defense. (Today's computer chips are manufactured in clean rooms that are much the same.)

Wrinkle-Free Cotton

Who invented it? Ruth Benerito
When? 1965
What? The use of cellulose chemistry to treat fabric so it doesn't form creases. (Stain- and flame-resistant fabrics later used the same method.)
Why? Saved time and money for home ironers.

*National Inventors Hall of Fame, 2021; years listed are for U.S. patent applications

What Are Some INVENTIONS of TODAY?*

Here are the whys behind some inventions of the late 20th and early 21st centuries.

Super Soaker

Who invented it? Lonnie Johnson
When? 1983
What? A squirt toy that shoots a continuous stream of water, inspired by the inventor's work on an environmentally friendly heat pump
Why? Fun! (Today's sales of the Super Soaker are well over $1 billion.)

Home Page Reader (HPR)

Who invented it? Chieko Asakawa
When? 2002
What? The first practical voice browser, using a numeric keypad instead of a computer mouse
Why? Provides effective internet access to blind and visually impaired people. (Today, web-to-speech browsers are commonplace around the world.)

Modified Messenger RNA (mRNA) Technology

Who invented it? Katalin Karikó and Drew Weissman
When? 2005
What? The discovery that modified mRNA can instruct the body's cells to make its own medicines, including COVID-19 vaccines
Why? Advances vaccines and treatments. Scientists are studying vaccines for rabies, malaria, and other diseases using mRNA.

Voice over Internet Protocol (VoIP) Technology

Who invented it? Marian Croak
When? 2009
What? The technology that converts voice into a digital signal that is transmitted over the internet
Why? Allows people to communicate through audio and/or video using the internet instead of a traditional phone line. (Today, Zoom calls use VoIP technology.)

*National Inventors Hall of Fame, 2021; years listed are for U.S. patent applications

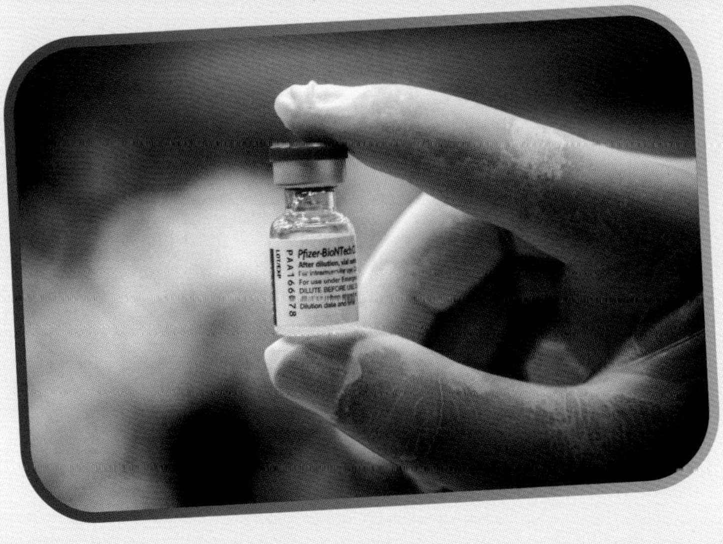

FUTURE WORLD

Will AI REPLACE human workers?

AI, or artificial intelligence, is a machine's capacity to perform tasks that humans usually do, such as understanding speech. But AI will not replace human workers. Humans are creative problem solvers. They connect and communicate personally with others, a skill essential for many jobs. And they are able to make critical decisions in the workplace. However, many industries, such as manufacturing and customer service, make use of AI-powered machines. Computers perform dangerous tasks in factories. They don't make mistakes nor do they tire or get bored. And they often operate at lower cost. One study predicts that when it comes to jobs worldwide, AI will eliminate 85 million—but create 97 million—by 2025. Someone has to program and run all those helpful automated computers.

What is 5G?

5G is the fifth-generation wireless technology. About every 10 years, a new wireless standard is released. 5G, first launched in some U.S. cities in 2019, is—surprise!—bigger and faster than 4G. One can already buy a 5G smartphone. Sports stadiums, gaming systems, and cars will rely on 5G technology. 5G might even lead to driverless cars and smart cities. 6G is expected to launch in 2030.

Might the INTERNET ever run out of SPACE?

Unlike the storage limits on individual devices, there is no limit to the size of the internet. It's just a way of connecting computers.

Will ROBOTS MAKE MY BED for me anytime soon?

Probably not. Robotic devices can scrub the BBQ grill, mow a lawn, and even clean the kitty litter. But a single so-called robot butler doing all household tasks as well as a human is a long way away. The robots are not safe or cheap enough to be practical. Prototypes cost about $75,000.

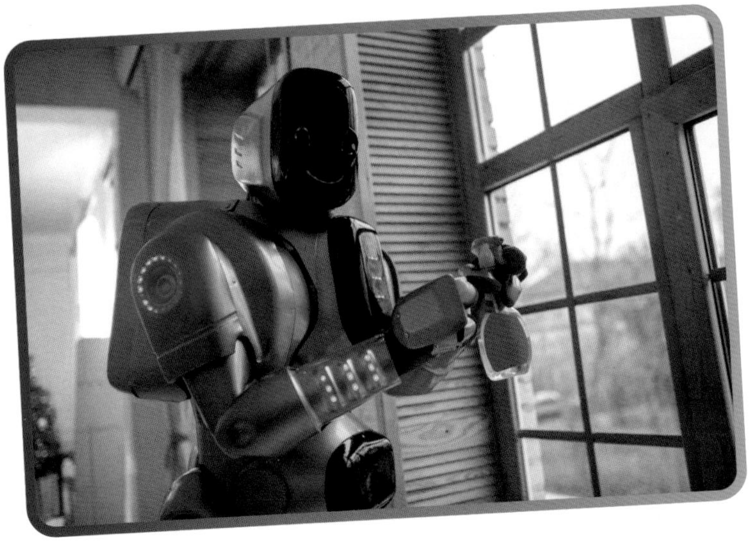

What will YOUTUBE VIDEOS of the future look like?

Who knows?! The first YouTube video was uploaded on April 23, 2005. The 18-second clip shows YouTube cofounder Jawed Karim at the San Diego Zoo, pointing out that elephants have long trunks. Today, YouTubers are producing more than 500 hours of content a minute. Can you imagine what life might be like in a 2055 YouTube video?

What kind of CLOTHES might we wear in the FUTURE?

Technological advances are a part of everything, even our clothing. Do any of these tech-wearables appeal to you? A jacket powered with solar panels to charge your device when you're on the go. Garments embedded with app-connected hardware. Exercise clothes with hidden sensors to track your workout and 3D imaging to help personalize your training. Or a smart belt that monitors and shares key health data during your day. A pair of powered self-lacing sneakers, anyone?

Learn More

Go to the National Inventors Hall of Fame to see the latest inductees and their inventions.

- www.invent.org/inductees/new-inductees

WE NEED
A CHANGE

WE THE PEOPLE

The words "We the People" appear in the preamble—the introduction—to the U.S. Constitution. Who are the people? What does a "perfect union" look like? How do we understand justice? For answers, look to your legislators (who pass the laws), your president, governor, and mayor (who carry out the laws), and your judges (who interpret the laws). Other questions are easier to resolve. Why do judges wear black robes? Do you pay for anything as president? Why are elections always held on Tuesdays? The results are in! It's a landslide of answers.

DON'T BE JUDGMENTAL

Why do judges use those WOODEN HAMMERS?

"Order in the court!" calls the judge. Then comes a *Bang! Bang!* on the desk with a wooden hammer, or gavel. Tapping the gavel is how judges on TV quiet the courtroom. In real life, most judges rely on their court officers to tell everyone to turn off their phones and settle down. Let the proceedings begin.

Why do judges wear BLACK ROBES?

Judges in England used to wear robes with different colors in court, along with long white wigs, which they still wear, uncomfortable and hot as they are. When John Marshall was sworn in as chief justice of the U.S. Supreme Court in 1801, he decided to wear a plain black robe (U.S. judges never required the wig). Today, an all-black robe is the tradition for U.S. judges. It highlights the belief that justice should be blind, or fair.

Can I visit the SUPREME COURT in session?

Yes. You can see the action for yourself in person, first-come, first-served. But not during COVID-19. The justices and lawyers participated remotely by telephone.

Learn More

Go to the Supreme Court of the United States to play audio recordings of actual oral arguments.

- www.supremecourt.gov/oral_arguments

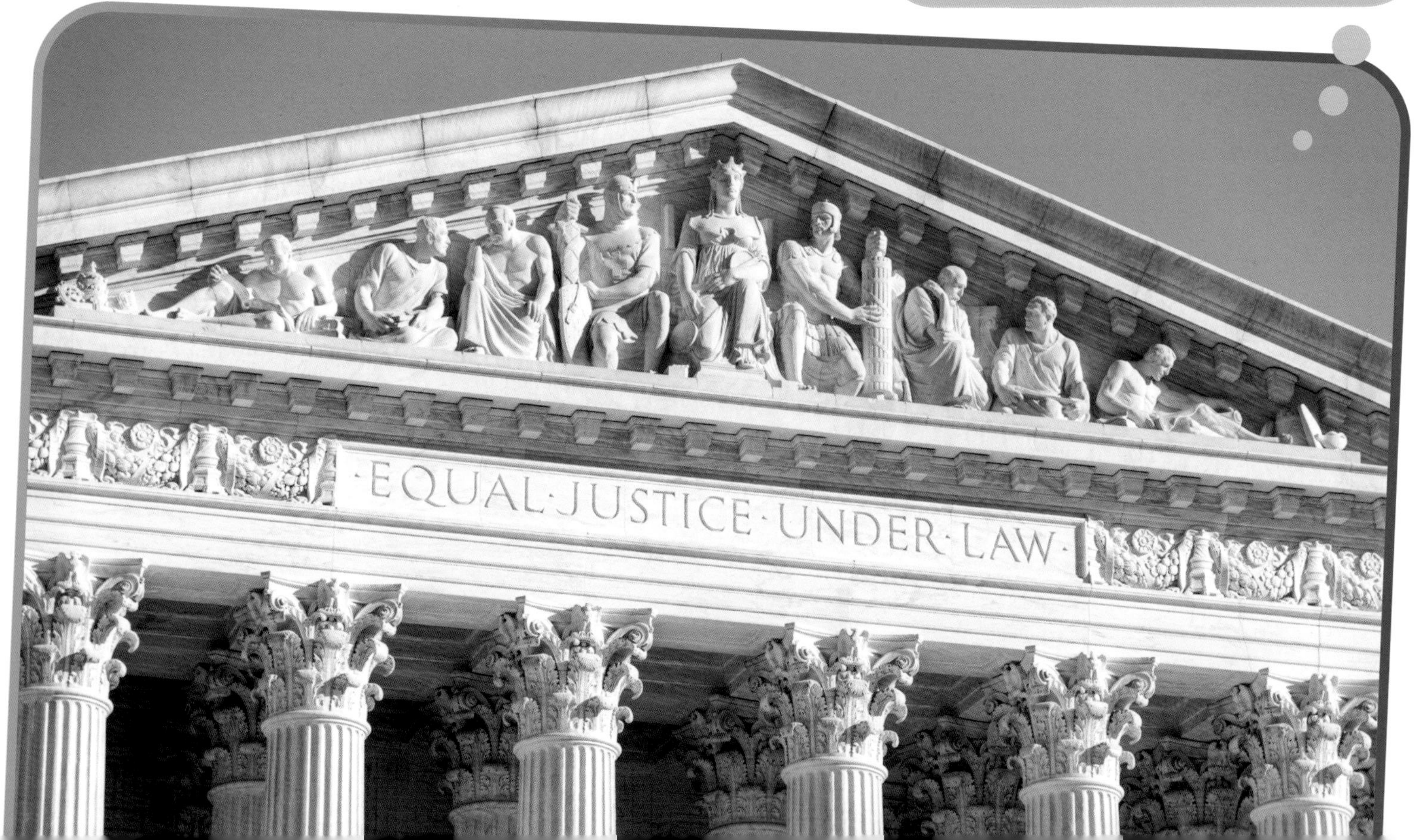

Why are there JURIES? (What are JURIES?)

U.S. citizens, if called, must serve on a jury. It's one way they participate in governing. A jury is a group of usually 12 people who decide a case that goes to trial. If someone is accused of a crime, they have the right to a jury trial. That right was set up in the Constitution's Bill of Rights.

Does everyone charged with a CRIME get a LAWYER?

If you are charged with a crime that might lead to prison time, you have the right to a lawyer even if you can't afford one.

Q&A: A Remarkable Person

Ruth Bader Ginsburg

Supreme Court Justice

When and where was she born? 1933, in Brooklyn, New York (she died in 2020)

How many women were in her 500-person class at Harvard Law? Nine total

What did she accomplish? Worked to strike down laws that treated men and women differently

How long did she serve on the Supreme Court? 27 years, until her death

What did she say? "Fight for the things that you care about, but do it in a way that will lead others to join you."

What's that thing COURT REPORTERS type on?

That tool is a stenotype machine. Court reporters, or stenographers, use it for a rapid writing called shorthand to record every word of a proceeding. By striking several of the machine's 22 keys at once, they can capture as many as 300 words a minute. Paired with a computer, the machine can deliver text in a real-time feed. But the official record doesn't include everything—like the noise of an apparent toilet flush during one live-streamed Supreme Court hearing in 2020!

Why do lawyers sometimes WORK FOR FREE?

The United States has more lawyers than any other nation in the world—one for every 240 Americans. But hiring one is very expensive—too expensive for many people to pay for. The American Bar Association—the professional organization overseeing lawyers—urges lawyers to work at least 50 hours a year *pro bono*. That's short for "for the public good" in Latin. It also gives lawyers a chance to develop new skills. And defending those without defenders is always the right thing to do.

STAND UP AND BE COUNTED

Who voted in the FIRST U.S. ELECTIONS?

In the early days of the country, not everyone could vote. The U.S. Constitution of 1787 didn't even mention the right to vote. Almost all voters were white men who owned land. Each state legislature controlled its own voting rules.

How did others get the RIGHT TO VOTE in the United States?

It took passage of the 15th Amendment to the U.S. Constitution in 1870 for Black men to have voting rights. And then passage of the 19th Amendment in 1920 to guarantee women the right to vote. Native Americans weren't allowed to vote until 1924. Later, in 1965, Congress passed the Voting Rights Act, outlawing practices that were in place to keep Black people, especially in the South, from casting ballots.

How many people VOTED in 2020?

More than 239 million people cast ballots in the 2020 presidential election. That's about 67 percent of eligible American voters. It was the highest percentage since 1900. But nearly 80 million people who could have voted did not participate.

Why Don't U.S. ADULTS Vote?*

REASON	PERCENT
Not registered to vote	29%
Not interested in politics	23%
Not liking the candidates	20%
A feeling their vote wouldn't have made a difference	16%
Being undecided about whom to vote for	10%

*NPR/Medill School of Journalism/Ipsos, 2020

Q&A: A Remarkable Person

John Lewis

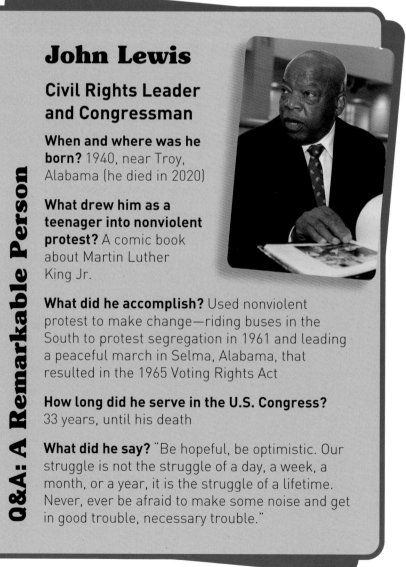

Civil Rights Leader and Congressman

When and where was he born? 1940, near Troy, Alabama (he died in 2020)

What drew him as a teenager into nonviolent protest? A comic book about Martin Luther King Jr.

What did he accomplish? Used nonviolent protest to make change—riding buses in the South to protest segregation in 1961 and leading a peaceful march in Selma, Alabama, that resulted in the 1965 Voting Rights Act

How long did he serve in the U.S. Congress? 33 years, until his death

What did he say? "Be hopeful, be optimistic. Our struggle is not the struggle of a day, a week, a month, or a year, it is the struggle of a lifetime. Never, ever be afraid to make some noise and get in good trouble, necessary trouble."

Why was the VOTING AGE lowered to 18?

The change in the voting age from 21 to 18 in 1971 was as simple as the slogan of the time—"Old enough to fight, old enough to vote." The U.S. government required men as young as 18 to sign up for military service until 1973.

What was the largest MOVEMENT in the United States?

In 2020, about 15 million to 26 million Americans participated in Black Lives Matter marches, protesting racial injustice. It is considered the largest movement in U.S. history.

Why do people MARCH as a form of PROTEST?

It's not just for the fresh air and exercise. Large outdoor marches raise public awareness and show support for historic issues. In 1963, some 250,000 people marched peacefully to the Lincoln Memorial in Washington, D.C., to protest racial inequalities. Martin Luther King Jr. gave his "I Have a Dream" speech there. One study found successful protests focus on three factors—organization, messaging, and nonviolence.

ELECTING TO VOTE

Why do we say "POLLS" and "POLLING STATIONS"?

In 13th-century England, the word *poll* meant "a head." Before paper ballots and secret voting, the easiest way to add up votes was counting people's heads. The place where votes were taken in this way became known as the polls.

Why is ELECTION DAY in early November?

In 1845, the U.S. Congress established an official Election Day. Before that, each state could choose any day before the first Wednesday in December. At that time, the voters—almost all men and white—were mainly farmers. Setting the election in early November was a good compromise. It came after the busy harvest season but before the depths of winter. After snow fell, travel by foot or on horseback to voting locations could be a challenge.

Is there a reason elections are almost always held on TUESDAYS?

Most Americans in the 19th century were Christians. Sundays would not have been acceptable because they were days of worship. Wednesdays were market days, when farmers gathered to sell their crops. As it often took overnight travel to get to the voting locations, that meant Monday and Thursday were out too. So Tuesday it was.

Why doesn't Election Day take place on the FIRST TUESDAY in November?

The answer to this question might not make much sense in the 21st century. But here goes. If the Tuesday Election Day happened to fall on the first day of November, there were three problems. First, for some Christians, November 1 is a holy day called All Saints' Day. Second, for merchants, the first day of the month was the day to settle accounts. Third, many members of Congress worried that poor economic results of the previous month might influence voters. So they chose the first Tuesday in November *after* the first Monday.

Why is Election Day **STILL ON TUESDAYS?**

What worked in 1845 doesn't work nearly as well today. Getting to the polls on a single day when many Americans have regularly scheduled work, school, and family commitments—or during a pandemic for that matter—is a tall order. In 2020, nearly two out of every three voters cast their ballots—by mail or early voting—before Election Day. But traditions can be hard to change.

Why is the **ELECTORAL COLLEGE** called a college?

The Electoral College is not an exact place or a school. The word *college* comes from the Latin *collegium* for "society." It has come to mean a group of people with the same responsibility. In this case, it's to formally elect the president. When Americans cast their votes for president, they are choosing their state's electors. Those electors, 538 in total, make up the Electoral College. A majority of 270 electoral votes are needed to win the presidency.

Why isn't the highest **POPULAR VOTE-GETTER** always the **WINNER** in presidential elections?

The Electoral College tips the scales a bit for the states with fewer voters. It is possible to win the most individual votes and still lose the electoral college, and election. In U.S. history, it has happened five times. In the 21st century, it's happened twice. In 2000, Al Gore was defeated by George W. Bush. And Hillary Clinton lost to Donald Trump in 2016.

ON THE CAMPAIGN TRAIL

Why do politicians **KISS BABIES?**

It's not hygienic. And it can look awkward. The first record of this often cringy custom was in 1833. A woman pushed her baby into the arms of President Andrew Jackson, campaigning in New Jersey. "A fine specimen of American childhood!" he reportedly said as he handed it off to his secretary of war for a peck. In 1984, Geraldine Ferraro—candidate for vice president and an experienced parent—wondered if offering babies to strangers for a germy embrace was a good idea. But she did it anyway. Politicians connect in a friendly way with voters by kissing their babies. Hey, every vote counts!

Do **TV POLITICAL DEBATES** change voters' minds?

They don't seem to have much effect. Some research says 72 percent of voters make up their minds more than two months before Election Day. That's often before the presidential debates even happen. And those who change their minds do so well after the debates.

How important is SOCIAL MEDIA in campaigns?

About one-fifth of U.S. adults say they get their political news mostly through social media. For those ages 18 to 29, it's almost half. Posts on social media are not checked for accuracy, of course, and they may have been put there to deliberately mislead voters. So beware!

How much MONEY does it take to RUN FOR OFFICE these days?

Save up your pennies! Spending in the 2020 election for president and Congress totaled more than $14 billion. It was the most expensive election by a large margin.

Why do candidates say "I APPROVE THIS MESSAGE" in political ads?

They have to. Congress passed the Stand by Your Ad provision in 2002. It holds candidates personally responsible for what they say in the radio and TV advertising that their campaign buys. But the law doesn't cover ads paid for by other organizations, or a candidate's digital ads, social media posts, or YouTube videos. All of these can be nasty, misleading, or false.

Make a Difference

The voting age in the United States is 18. Some states allow 16-year-olds to preregister to vote. In the meantime, talk to voters in your life about the issues and upcoming elections. Be informed. Ask questions. Don't reshare inaccurate information.

PRIMARILY PRESIDENTIAL

Why is the OVAL OFFICE oval?

The White House was built in 1800. Its first resident was second president John Adams. At that time, the building contained three oval-shaped reception rooms. The shape allowed special guests—usually men—to assemble in a circle while the president acknowledged them one by one. Although this practice soon fell out of fashion (third president Thomas Jefferson didn't like the formality), the current office of the U.S. president, built in 1909, retains this oval shape as a tribute to the past.

Do you PAY FOR ANYTHING as president?

Yes. As president, you earn a salary of $400,000 a year. And you may live in the White House and fly in your own plane, but not everything is free. U.S. presidents pay for their own food (though not the chef who prepares it), most of their clothing, dry cleaning, and hairstyling, among other things. You know what they say, there's no such thing as a free lunch.

What is the MAXIMUM NUMBER of years a U.S. president can serve?

Franklin D. Roosevelt was elected for four terms and served 12 years—from 1933 until his death in 1945. Since then, no one has held the position longer than eight years. That's because of the 22nd Amendment to the Constitution, which was added in 1951. It limits presidents to only two four-year terms, plus as many as two years of the previous president's term in the case of death, resignation, or removal from office. That's a possible total of 10 years. The presidential term limit is a check on presidential power.

Is the president allowed to DRIVE?

The Secret Service is the federal agency responsible for protecting political leaders and their families. That means U.S. presidents, past and present, are not allowed to drive a car on public streets. They may only ride in a highly secured vehicle, operated by a driver who is trained for all emergency situations.

What's so special about AIR FORCE ONE?

Officially, any plane carrying the U.S. president is called Air Force One. That's the air traffic call sign. But most of the time, the president travels by air in one of two highly customized jets. Each one contains a presidential suite with a gym, two kitchens, and a conference room. There are also work and rest areas for the press, plane crew, and presidential staff. There's even an onboard doctor ready to perform surgery—and the equipment they would need to do that—in an emergency. The aircraft's range is almost 8,000 miles (12,000 km). But Air Force One is capable of refueling in the air so it could circle the globe continuously. If the United States were ever attacked while the president was in flight, Air Force One functions as a mobile command center.

Learn More

Go to WH.gov to find out about the current administration, past presidents, and the official residence.

- www.whitehouse.gov

CUSTOMS AND CONVENTIONS

Why do presidents use so many PENS to sign DOCUMENTS?

Sometimes it looks as though someone's playing a trick on the president. Why don't any of these pens work? But it's just part of a long political tradition. Signing a historic bill with several official pens—and then giving them away as keepsakes—allows the president to honor the supporters who worked to pass the legislation. President Lyndon Johnson signed the Civil Rights Act in 1964 with 75 pens. The only challenge is writing slowly enough to be able to use all the pens!

Why do politicians cut RIBBONS?

Ribbon-cutting ceremonies began as part of wedding celebrations in Europe. Cutting a ribbon across the door of the family home symbolized a fresh start. The first recorded ribbon-cutting ceremony to introduce a new business in the United States took place in 1898 in Union Parish, Louisiana. It marked the launch of railroad service to the city. Since then, politicians around the country have cut ribbons at grand openings for local businesses. And they always take out the huge scissors for celebrations of new public libraries, schools, and parks.

Do POETS always speak at presidential INAUGURATIONS?

Only four presidents—John F. Kennedy, Bill Clinton, Barack Obama, and Joe Biden—have included poets at their swearing-in ceremonies. Amanda Gorman, at age 22, became the youngest. She recited her poem "The Hill We Climb" at Biden's inauguration in January 2021. A few weeks later, Gorman performed before the Super Bowl coin toss—the first poet ever to do so.

Why do mayors give **KEYS TO THE CITY?**

Long ago, cities had walls around them to protect their citizens. The gates were guarded during the day and locked at night. Trusted visitors were sometimes presented with a key to the city gate so they could enter freely. Today, mayors often present local heroes with oversized keys that don't open anything. For example, Captain Chesley Sullenberger got a key to New York City in 2009. That was for landing a disabled plane full of people safely—on the Hudson River!

Is it true **BEAN SOUP** has been on the Senate menu every day since 1904?

No. One day in the 1940s during World War II, the cooks ran out of their ration of beans and were unable to serve it. And it's likely days of bean soup were missed during the COVID-19 shutdown in 2020.

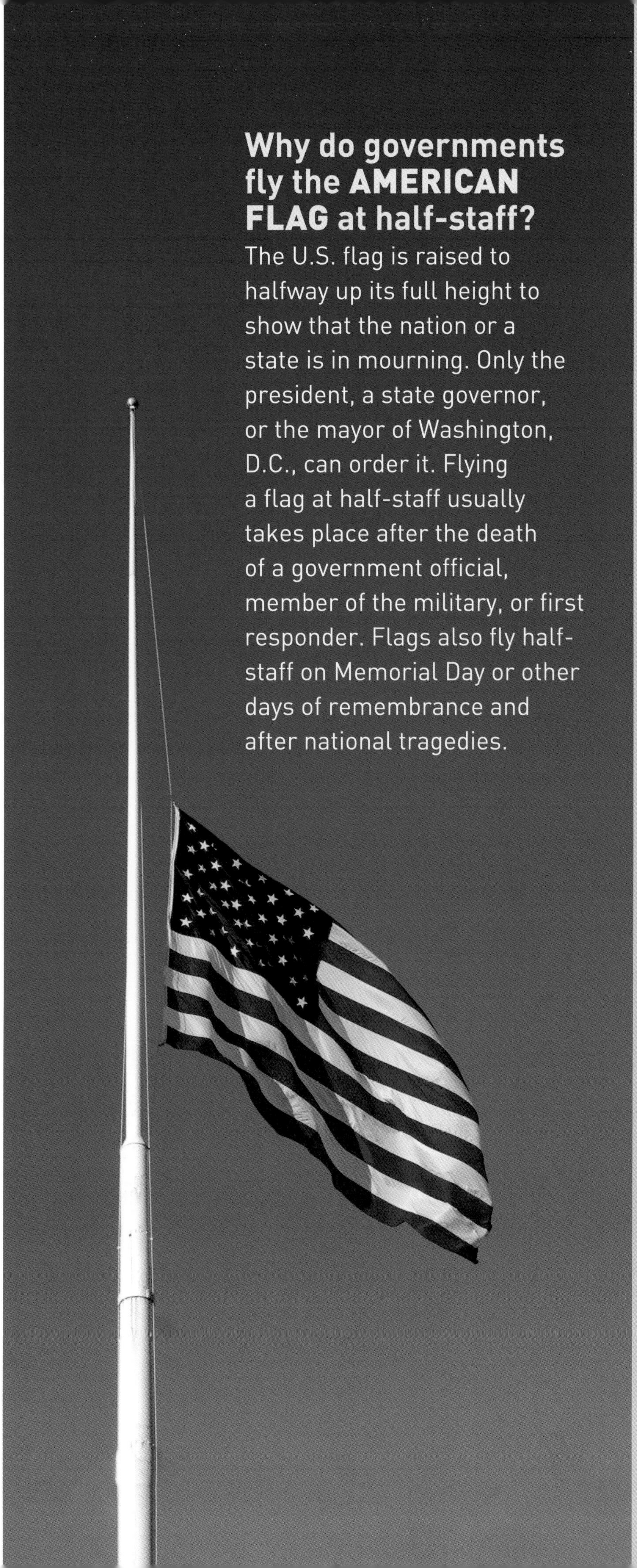

Why do governments fly the **AMERICAN FLAG** at half-staff?

The U.S. flag is raised to halfway up its full height to show that the nation or a state is in mourning. Only the president, a state governor, or the mayor of Washington, D.C., can order it. Flying a flag at half-staff usually takes place after the death of a government official, member of the military, or first responder. Flags also fly half-staff on Memorial Day or other days of remembrance and after national tragedies.

GOVERNMENT ACTS

Who decides what goes on U.S. POSTAGE STAMPS?

The U.S. postmaster general has appointed the Citizens' Stamp Advisory Committee since 1957. The committee offers recommendations to the postmaster general for final approval. But there are rules. Stamps must feature American or American-related subjects, or themes of widespread national appeal. They honor contributions to American society, history, culture, or environment. No living person will be considered. A memorial stamp is automatically issued after the death of a president. If you have an interesting stamp idea, you can download the guidelines to submit it from the U.S. Postal Service website, USPS.com. But you'll have to print it out, and mail it in, naturally.

What do TAXES pay for?

The government collects different kinds of taxes to fund services you might not even notice. Most of the national budget goes toward the military and national defense, Social Security—that's monthly payments for retired people—and major health programs. The U.S. government usually spends more than $4 trillion a year. That's a lot of bucks to balance, but it doesn't even include the taxes collected by state and other local governments.

Why do cities and towns provide TRASH PICKUP?

Regular trash removal keeps communities clean and safe. This government service helps reduce flies and rodent infestations. These days, automated trucks, larger trash containers, and expanded recycling programs make trash collecting easier. But it's probably no less smelly. Would you believe public garbage trucks in New York City collect almost 7,700 tons (6,985 mt) of mixed solid waste from residents every day?

What Are the Top Five CHALLENGES the Government Handles Well?*

TASK	PERCENT OF AMERICANS WHO SAY SOMEWHAT GOOD OR VERY GOOD
Keeping country safe from terrorism	72%
Responding to natural disasters	62%
Ensuring safe food and medicine	62%
Strengthening economy	54%
Maintaining infrastructure	53%

*Pew Research Center, 2020

Learn More

Go to USA.gov to find your U.S. senators, U.S. representative, governor, state legislators, and local elected officials.

- www.usa.gov/elected-officials

Why is a SOCIAL SECURITY number nine digits?

Having nine digits allows for quite a few number combinations—almost 1 billion! More than 450 million numbers have been issued by the Social Security Administration since 1936. The numbers are randomly assigned and never reused. These identification cards help track someone's earning history to determine their benefits when they retire.

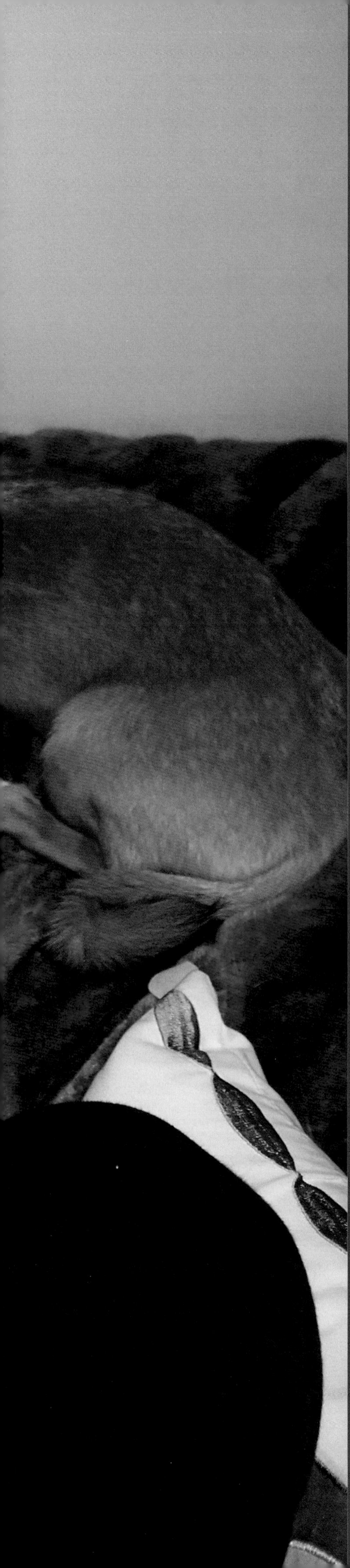

WHAT'S POPULAR

Pop—or popular—culture is everywhere. It's what everyone is doing, even if we do our own thing too. We eat our snacks and gulp our drinks. We throw on our clothes. We choose what to read and watch. We enjoy games. We use slang. We listen and move our bodies to the latest music. In the world of what's popular, there are questions everyone's asking. Why do people dance on TikTok? Who invented sweatpants? Which pop musicians have won the most Grammys? Why do we eat popcorn at the movies? Let's get some answers. It'll be epic.

YUM-YUM!

What is the most popular AMERICAN SNACK FOOD?

In a 2021 survey, M&M's, Reese's Peanut Butter Cups, and Ritz crackers topped the list of the most popular food and snack brands in the United States. Quaker oatmeal came in at number five, with Lay's potato chips at number eight. Celery and carrots did not make the list, but maybe they could, with a little branding.

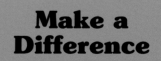

Why are so many people VEGAN?

About 3 percent of Americans—and possibly you—are vegans. Vegans eat food from plants, such as fruit, vegetables, nuts, seeds, lentils, and beans. They don't eat foods that come from animals. That includes milk, eggs, cheese, and even honey. Eating vegan avoids harming any animals. It can help the environment too. And there are more options for plant-based foods every year. Vegan-friendly burgers, cheeses, snacks—and even ice cream—are now widely on sale.

Does ginger ale actually have GINGER in it?

Lawsuits have been recently settled over misleading advertising from ginger ale companies. There are some health benefits from consuming ginger root. Studies say it helps treat upset stomachs and nausea. But today's ginger ales often don't contain much or any natural ginger. In fact, a glass of ginger ale can have as many as 10 teaspoons (42 g) of sugar. That can make your upset stomach even worse. Why not just go back to bed?

Make a Difference

Help your friends or siblings make a meal for the family. Go to Cooking with Kids to find ideas and how-to videos.

- cookingwithkids.org

Why are most pizzas ROUND? Why are they about the SAME SIZE?

Many pizza pros stretch pizza dough by spinning a ball of it in the air. That spinning action forms a circle. It's an example of centrifugal force, which causes something rotating around a center to move away from the center. In 1984, a trade association in Naples, Italy, first defined an authentic Neapolitan pizza. It can measure no wider than 13.8 inches (35 cm) and must bake directly on the oven stone, in no longer than 90 seconds.

Which PIZZA TOPPINGS Are the TOPS?*

Most LIKED Toppings

TOPPING	PERCENT
Pepperoni	64%
Sausage	56%
Mushrooms	54%
Extra cheese	52%
Onions	48%

Most DISLIKED Toppings

TOPPING	PERCENT
Anchovies	61%
Eggplant	52%
Artichokes	44%
Broccoli	39%
Pineapple	35%

*YouGovAmerica, 2021

COMING TO A THEATER NEAR YOU

Why do BIG FILMS usually open on FRIDAYS?

Box office numbers—the amount a movie makes from ticket sales—for the opening weekend are crucial for a movie to succeed financially. The practice of opening on a Friday began with *Gone with the Wind*. The epic romance, which opened on Friday, December 15, 1939, was an immediate blockbuster. Sometimes a highly anticipated movie with dedicated fans opens on a Thursday or even Wednesday. That helps create buzz to boost numbers over the weekend and beyond.

Why do we eat POPCORN at the movies?

Popcorn kernels are inexpensive to buy and pop. Considered street food, popcorn was mostly sold at carnivals and fairs and wasn't allowed into early elegant movie palaces. So vendors sold bags of it for 5 or 10 cents outside the theaters. To attract customers during the Great Depression of the 1930s, theater owners finally permitted the hot buttered snack inside. By 1945, Americans ate more than half their popcorn at the cinema. Today, almost half of the overall profits of movie theaters come from the concession stand.

Q&A: A Remarkable Person

Emma Watson

Actor and Activist

When was she born and where was she raised? 1990, in Oxfordshire, UK

What was her first professional acting job? Playing Hermione Granger in *Harry Potter and the Sorcerer's Stone* (she was 10)

What other movies has she appeared in? *Beauty and the Beast* (2017) and *Little Women* (2019)

What else has she accomplished? Named a United Nations Women's Goodwill Ambassador, which fights discrimination against women worldwide

What has she said? "In my moments of doubt I've told myself firmly—if not me, who, if not now, when. If you have similar doubts when opportunities are presented to you, I hope those words might be helpful."

Why are **MOVIES** so **COSTLY** to make?

In the modern film industry, it seems you have to spend money to make money. Story rights, the screenplay, producers, and an experienced director are expensive. And A-list stars demand even more. Then there are the production costs, special effects, and music. For a potential hit, film distributors often spend more than $100 million on advertising alone. But then, it's probably never been cheaper to make and edit your own film. You can do it on your phone.

What Were the Ten MOST EXPENSIVE Movies?*

FILM	COST
Pirates of the Caribbean: On Stranger Tides (2011)	$422 million
Avengers: Age of Ultron (2015)	$386 million
Pirates of the Caribbean: At World's End (2007)	$362 million
Avengers: Endgame (2019)	$356 million
Avengers: Infinity War (2018)	$316 million
Titanic (1997)	$312 million
Spider-Man 3 (2007)	$312 million
Justice League (2017)	$307 million
Tangled (2010)	$299 million
Harry Potter and the Half-Blood Prince (2009)	$292 million

*NerdWallet, 2020; adjusted for inflation

Learn More

Go to the Academy of Motion Picture Arts and Sciences to find the latest award winners.

- www.oscars.org

SICK BEATS

Why do singers wear those EARPIECES on stage?

Those in-ear monitors give singers one consistent source of sound. They protect the singer's hearing from often ear-splittingly loud music. In-ear monitors also allow the wearer to listen to backing tracks the audience can't hear. For example, hearing only the drum can help keep a singer on the right beat. Rock on.

Who was the first HIP-HOP performer?

Clive Campbell, better known as DJ Kool Herc. One night in 1974, the 18-year-old from Jamaica appeared at a club in New York City's South Bronx. He spun two copies of the same record, mixing the sounds and extending the drum beats. The audience loved it. They were able to dance longer to their favorite parts of the song. By the 1990s, hip-hop was a global phenomenon.

Why is it called K-POP?

K-pop is short for "Korean popular music." The original K-pop stars, the Kim Sisters, appeared on *Billboard*'s singles chart in 1962. In 2012, Korean singer Psy had the then-most viewed YouTube video of all-time with "Gangnam Style." In 2020, BTS became the first Korean group to take the number-one spot on the *Billboard* Hot 100. At the same time, BTS's "Dynamite" broke the record for most viewed YouTube video in 24 hours—more than 101 million.

Why does CLASSICAL training help pop singers?
For all singers, their body is an instrument. Classical training makes the most of that instrument. Singers learn how to stand and warm up their voices. They support their breathing for the fullest sound. They develop their vocal range and phrasing. But the proof is in the pudding. Billie Eilish began singing in a choral group at age eight. Jason Derulo studied musical theater in high school. Charlie Puth graduated from a music college. And Lady Gaga is a classical pianist. Drop the mic.

Which (Nonclassical) Musicians Have Won the Most GRAMMYS?*

MUSICIAN	NUMBER
Beyoncé	28
Quincy Jones	28
Alison Krauss	27
Stevie Wonder	25
Chick Corea	25
Jay-Z	23
U2	22
Vince Gill	22
Kanye West	22

*Grammy Awards, 2021

Learn More

Go to the Recording Academy to find past and present Grammy Award winners and videos.

- www.grammy.com

Q&A: A Remarkable Person

Nandi Bushell

Drummer and YouTuber

When and where was she born? 2010, in Durban, South Africa (she lives in Ipswich, UK)

What inspired her at age five to ask for a drum kit? Watching Beatles drummer Ringo Starr in a "Hey Jude" video

What does she do? Covers rock songs on her YouTube channel (managed by her parents)

What else has she accomplished? Beat Dave Grohl of Foo Fighters in a virtual drum battle

What has she said? "I feel proud of myself and honored to know that people like watching my videos and feel happy watching them."

SLICK MOVES

Is **BREAK DANCING** considered a sport?

Break dancing is a hip-hop dance form. It involves fancy footwork and athletic moves such as back and head spins. This dancing is in fact so athletic, it is considered a competitive sport. The International Olympic Committee announced in 2020 that break dancers, often called b-boys or b-girls, may participate in the next Summer Games, in France.

Why is it called the **FLOSS DANCE**?

A 14-year-old named Russell Horning first posted this quirky dance move on Instagram in 2016. It involves swinging both arms in a motion that mimics flossing teeth. The next year, he performed with Katy Perry on TV. Some viewers thought the video of his dancing was sped up. It wasn't.

Why do people DANCE ON TIKTOK?

TikTok is the place for the latest dance moves and choreographed routines. Where else would you learn how to hit the woah? That's making a quick circular motion with your fists and freezing on the beat. TikTok's origins and structure have made it the perfect app for viral dances. When TikTok launched in 2016, it was a music-focused app called Musical.ly. It's hard to dance without music! At only 15 seconds, the first TikToks had time just for a few slick moves. The vertical frame of a TikTok video is great for capturing a single person dancing. Many TikToks share the user's personal vibe as much as their dance skills.

Q&A: A Remarkable Person

Alvin Ailey

Modern Dance Company Founder

When and where was he born? 1931, in Rogers, Texas (he died in 1989)

What were his childhood pastimes? Drawing insects, writing poetry, and playing the tuba

What inspired him in his choreography? Memories of get-down dancing on Saturday nights at the local inn and blues, spirituals, and gospel music from his childhood church

What did he accomplish? Founded his own, mostly Black, international dance company, in 1958

How many ballets did he choreograph? 79

What did he say? "Dance is for everybody. I believe that dance came from the people and that it should always be delivered back to the people."

How did the first FLASH MOB happen?

Flash mobs are sudden gatherings of people organized through texting or the internet. The group carries out an activity, sometimes dancing, in a public place, then quickly disperses. The first flash mob took place in 2003. A *Harper's Magazine* editor named Bill Wasik emailed friends to gather in a New York City shop. But someone tipped off the police, and only about 20 of them got into the store. Within days, flash mobs were happening in other cities. Wasik viewed his flash mob as a kind of performance art that could show "what technology can do." These days, smaller flash mobs of friends dancing appear on social media.

WORD

What is SLANG?

People use words to communicate, as we all know. Subcultures—ethnic groups or gamers or musicians or young people—often converse in their own words and phrases. These informal, conversational words are called slang. Over time, slang words can become standard vocabulary.

What Does That MEAN?*

Some slang terms stick around a long time. Other phrases quickly seem outdated. Here are some examples of both.

DECADE	SLANG	MEANING
1910s	duck soup	an easy task
1920s	the bee's knees	outstanding
1930s	a gig	a job
1940s	sitting in the hot seat	in an uncomfortable or embarrassing situation
1950s	a boo-boo	a mistake; a wound
1960s	the Man	a group in power
1970s	Catch you on the flip side!	See you later!
1980s	Gag me with a spoon.	That's disgusting.
1990s	phat	cool or hip
2000s	rents	parents
2010s	photobombing	moving into the frame of a picture as it is being taken, as a joke or prank

*Editors of Publications International, 2021

THE WHYS BEHIND WORDS OF THE YEAR

Every year, Collins Dictionary, founded in 1819, selects the most popular word. It takes into consideration online, TV, radio, book, newspaper, and conversational use. Here are the whys behind some of those words.

Lockdown

When? 2020

What does it mean? The imposition of stringent restrictions on travel, social interaction, and access to public spaces

Why? More than 250,000 usages of the word, up from 4,000 the previous year; the word "encapsulates the shared experience of billions of people" during the coronavirus pandemic

Climate Strike

When? 2019

What does it mean? A form of protest in which people absent themselves from education or work in order to join demonstrations demanding action to counter climate change

Why? Usage of the word increased 100-fold from the previous year; in 2018, Swedish 15-year-old Greta Thunberg skipped school to protest for more action against climate change, holding a sign that read "School Strike for Climate"

Single-Use

When? 2018

What does it mean? Made to be used once only before being thrown away (often referring to plastic)

Why? Usage of the word increased four-fold since 2013; the word "encompasses a global movement to kick our addiction to disposable products"

Fake News

When? 2017

What does it mean? False, often sensational, information disseminated under the guise of news reporting

Why? Usage of the term increased by 365 percent since previous year; the term has contributed to "the undermining of society's trust in news reporting"

LIFE'S A GAME

Why is it so hard to solve a RUBIK'S CUBE?

Maybe because there are 43 quintillion possible configurations of the standard 3x3x3 cube. Even Erno Rubik, the Hungarian architect who invented the multicolored puzzle toy in 1974, took a month to solve it. Since then, mathematicians have proved you can solve any configuration in 20 moves or fewer. That's how the world's fastest cubers solve it in less than five seconds. They've learned step-by-step rules—called algorithms—to twist the 26 small cubes into the right positions.

Are there really 1,000 pieces in a 1,000-PIECE PUZZLE?

Jigsaw puzzles are usually arranged in a rectangular grid, making it hard to end up with exactly 1,000 pieces. The most common layout for a 1,000-piece puzzle, for example, is 38 pieces by 27 pieces. That's a total of 1,026. Hey, that's 26 pieces for free!

What Are the ALL-TIME Bestselling VIDEO GAMES?*

TITLE	ESTIMATED COPIES
Tetris (1984)	500 million
Minecraft (2011)	238 million
Grand Theft Auto V (2013)	150 million
Wii Sports (2006)	82.9 million
PlayerUnknown's Battlegrounds (2017)	70 million

*Screen Rant, 2021

Learn More

Go to the Strong National Museum of Play for information about video games by decade.

- www.museumofplay.org/about/icheg/video-game-history/timeline

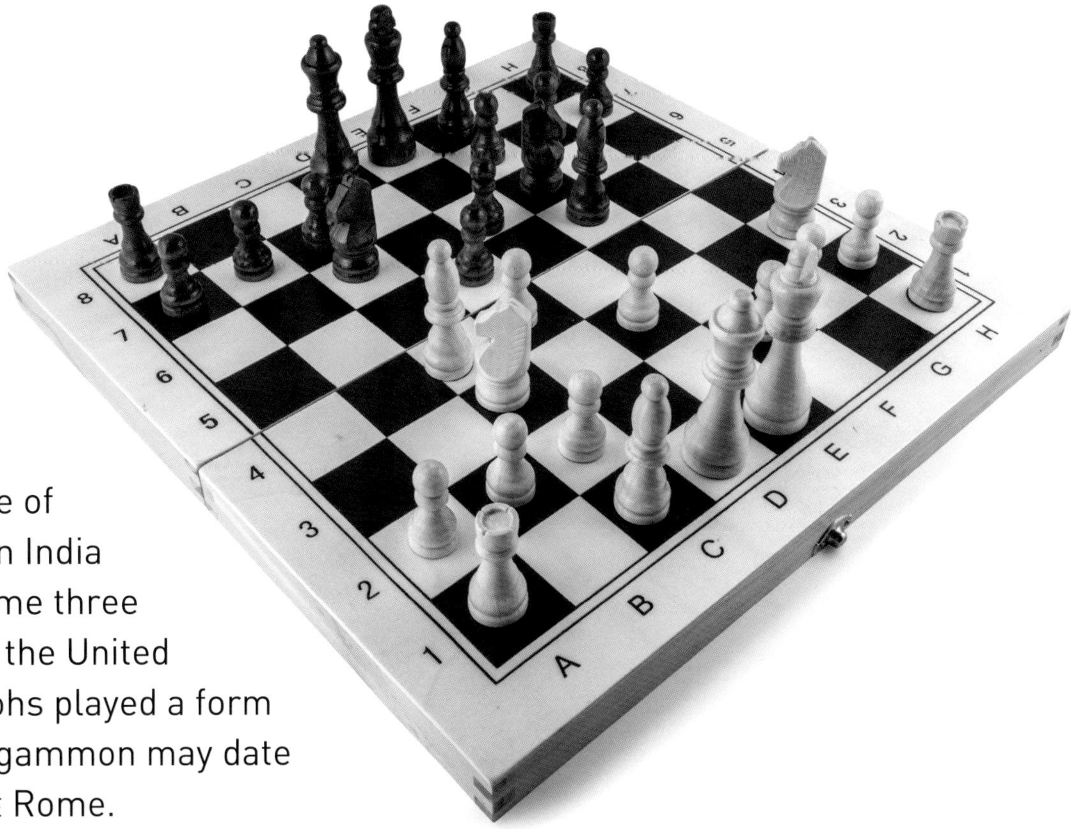

What are the bestselling **BOARD GAMES?**

The top three all-time bestselling board games are some of the oldest. Chess originated in India in about the sixth century. Some three million sets sell every year in the United States alone. Egyptian pharaohs played a form of checkers in 1600 BCE. Backgammon may date back even further, to 3000 BCE Rome.

What's the **BESTSELLING** board game sold by a single company?

Monopoly is the world's bestselling trademarked board game. It is sold in 114 countries and in 47 languages. Parker Brothers introduced the game in 1935. Monopoly is based on the Landlord's Game. It was created by a woman named Elizabeth Phillips in 1904 to highlight the plight of the American poor in the "present system of land-grabbing." Since then, more than one billion people have played the game.

Why are there two **JOKERS** in a pack of cards?

Euchre, a popular card game from 19th-century France, requires a joker to play. That's why jokers are included in a standard pack. A joker can also replace any lost card or serve as a wild card in other games.

Make a Difference

Organize a game night for your family. Or opt for a quieter activity and set up a puzzle for family members to work on together. Choose something that might appeal to everyone in your home.

A REAL PAGE-TURNER

How are GRAPHIC NOVELS different from COMIC BOOKS?

A graphic novel is published as—and reads like—a book. Characters develop through the narrative's beginning, middle, and end. The term *graphic novel* can also include short stories and writing that is factual. A comic book is short and is printed regularly, often every month or even every week. It has plots that carry over to the next issue. Sales of graphic novels and comics (digital and print) reached nearly $1.3 billion in North America in 2020. That's a lot of dope art and cool stories.

What is MANGA? Why is it printed right to left?

Japanese comic books and graphic novels are called *manga*. It means "whimsical pictures" in Japanese. Manga follows *tategaki*, meaning you read right to left and top down. When you hold manga, the spine is on the right. Unlike English-language comic books, manga is most often in black and white. It is faster to produce and considered more artistic by many artists and fans.

What Are the All-Time BESTSELLING NOVELS?*

TITLE	AUTHOR	ESTIMATED COPIES
Don Quixote	Miguel de Cervantes	500 million
A Tale of Two Cities	Charles Dickens	200 million
The Fellowship of the Ring	J. R. R. Tolkien	150 million
The Little Prince	Antoine de Saint-Exupéry	140 million
Harry Potter and the Sorcerer's Stone	J. K. Rowling	120 million

*Business Insider, 2021

Are AUTOBIOGRAPHIES and MEMOIRS the same?

No. A memoir is a collection of the writer's memories, usually about a specific time or experience. An autobiography is the writer's entire life story. *The Story of My Life* by Helen Keller is an example of an autobiography. Trevor Noah's *Born a Crime: Stories from a South African Childhood* is a memoir.

Make a Difference

Check to see if your local public library takes book donations. Look for schools or other organizations that might need used picture books. Collect some volumes that your family and friends are ready to pass on to new readers. Lead a book drive at your school.

Q&A: A Remarkable Person

Jeff Kinney

Children's Author and Illustrator

When and where was he born? 1971, in Fort Washington, Maryland

What were his favorite books as a child? *Freckle Juice* by Judy Blume, *The Hobbit* by J. R. R. Tolkien, and *The Lion, the Witch, and the Wardrobe* by C. S. Lewis

What has he accomplished? Written and illustrated the Diary of a Wimpy Kid series, which by 2021 had sold more than 250 million copies in 65 different languages

What else does he do? Runs a bookstore called An Unlikely Story in Plainville, Massachusetts, and works for Poptropica, a story-based gaming website

What has he said? "Most of my latest book was written longhand, in messy handwriting and violent strike-throughs. I've got whole pages where there are only two or three usable words. But I got the job done, and I made another deadline."

CALLING ALL FASHIONISTAS

Who invented SWEATPANTS?

A Frenchman, Emile Camuset, designed the first casual knitted pants for athletes in the 1920s. Customers appreciated his comfortable sportswear. They found the gray pants absorbed perspiration during exercise. Maybe that's why they're called sweatpants. Some one hundred years later, clothing sales had their largest drop ever—79 percent. It was April 2020, the first full month of the pandemic. However, sales of sweatpants, the perfect stay-at-home fashion, were up 80 percent.

Why are they called SNEAKERS?

Tennis shoes are made of canvas with a pliable rubber sole. They are often worn for other sports or just around town. The word *sneakers* came into use in the 1880s. The rubber soles were quiet enough the wearer could sneak around without being noticed. Or so they say.

Why do BLUE JEANS have those small pockets inside the front pocket?

That tiny pocket is called a watch pocket. It was originally designed for men to store their—you guessed it—watches! In fact, those timepieces were called pocket watches, because, well, you get the idea.

Make a Difference

Collect clothing for local shelters. Or donate a bag of clothing you've outgrown to a charitable organization. There are many ways to recycle.

THE WHYS BEHIND SOME FASHION TRENDS

People of all ages express themselves in what they choose to wear. Here are the whys behind some trends.

Baseball Caps
How? Tie-dye, vintage, or corduroy
Why? A fun hat tops off a relaxed but put-together look.

Simple T-shirts
How? Black or white
Why? These staples are comfortable, always stylish, and versatile.

Colorful Socks
How? Embroidered or patterned
Why? This small fashion detail brings personal style to a drab outfit.

Second-Hand Clothing
How? Oversized, unique, and often high quality
Why? Everyone appreciates recycling. And the prices can't be beat.

How do FASHION TRENDS start?

Fashion trends traditionally start with imaginative fashion designers. They create looks for fashion runways and high-end brands. Those trends then get adapted as they trickle down to retail stores—that's why it seems like every store might be selling plaid prints one year and animal prints the next. Celebrities can be fashion pioneers. Musicians, athletes, actors, and social media influencers shape what people want to wear. (Think NBA stars making game day entrances in designer suits and other high fashion.) Other times, the coolest looks come from street style. That's the wacky, retro, or spontaneous style adaptations of regular people. And then there's trendcasting. That's collecting and analyzing data on buying habits and current culture to forecast the future. What's the next fashion-forward fad?

INDEX

Q

R

S

T

U

V

W

Y

FIND OUT FOR YOURSELF!

WRITE DOWN YOUR OWN HOWS, WHATS, WHENS, AND WHYS . . .

WHO? WHAT? WHERE?

WHEN? HOW? WHY?